UNIVERSITY OF NORTH CAROLINA
STUDIES IN THE ROMANCE LANGUAGES AND LITERATURES
Number 54

STUDIES IN ROMANCE LEXICOLOGY, BASED ON
A COLLECTION OF LATE LATIN DOCUMENTS
FROM RAVENNA (AD 445-700)

STUDIES IN ROMANCE LEXICOLOGY,
BASED ON A COLLECTION OF LATE LATIN DOCUMENTS FROM RAVENNA (AD 445-700)

BY

CHARLES MERRITT CARLTON

CHAPEL HILL
THE UNIVERSITY OF NORTH CAROLINA PRESS

DEPÓSITO LEGAL: V. 2.652 — 1965

ARTES GRÁFICAS SOLER, S. A. — VALENCIA — 1965

PREFACE

The current study is a revised and somewhat expanded version of a portion of a doctoral dissertation, *A Linguistic Analysis of a Collection of Late Latin Documents Composed in Ravenna between AD 445-700* (University of Michigan, 1963). Our corpus consisted of a collection of documents published by Dr. Jan-Olof Tjäder in his critical edition, *Die nichtliterarischen lateinischen Papyri Italiens aus der Zeit 445-700,* vol. I, Lund, 1955.

While much of the original work had a statistical orientation, following models provided by R. L. and F. N. Politzer, and Mario Pei (see Bibliography), and touched on Phonology, Morphology, and Syntax, it ultimately became clear that *from the standpoint of the Romance languages* it was the lexicon which offered us the greatest interest.

Our additions and emendations reflect for the most part further corroboration and attestation of forms cited in works which were unavailable to us earlier. In two cases only (*punga* and *feria*) were we obliged to alter our earlier presentation in any substantial way. This of course does not mean to say that the history of the words we have treated has as yet been exhaustively handled, for while we have availed ourselves of 24 new sources, full coverage of the various problems encountered must necessarily await completion of the many studies which are still appearing in serialized form (e. g., Arnaldi). The *Mittellateinisches Wörterbuch* is the only work to which we referred earlier (in the case of *ager*) and for which another fascicle has since appeared (concerning *armarium*). Completion of the Niermeyer work (now through *sequipeda*), especially with an indication of the abbreviations employed, works cited, etc., would obviously facilitate our task.

The *Słownik łaciny...* has appeared thus far through *confrontaneus*. Other works, too, will no doubt prove one day to be of value, but thus far certain of them have not appeared sufficiently advanced in terms of publication for us to be able to judge (e. g., *Glossarium mediae Latinitatis Cataloniae, voces latinas y romances documentadas en fuentes catalanas, del año 800 al 1100*, Barcelona, 1961—, thus far: *a* to *bene*, and *Diccionario histórico de la lengua española, Seminario de lexicografía*, of the Real Academia Española, Madrid, 1960—, *a* to *abundar*).

Finally we point to the possibility of research yet to be undertaken in the Ravenna collection, since our work has been based on approximately half of the documents (28 out of 55) which Tjäder had at his disposal.

We acknowledge our debt to the excellent and copious notes provided by Tjäder, and we express also our sincere thanks to Professor Hans E. Keller, now of the University of Utrecht, who guided our original study.

TABLE OF CONTENTS

	Page
PREFACE	7
BRIEF NOTE CONCERNING THE CORPUS	11
A. INTRODUCTION	13
B. STARRED ITEMS AND "CAPSICIUS"	14
C. SINGLE ITEMS RESTRICTED IN DISTRIBUTION IN THE ROMANIA	16

1.1. Italy
    a. *runcilio* ... 16
    b. *armarium* ... 17
    c. *necessus* ... 19
    d. *horticellus* ... 21
    e. *cata* ... 21

1.2. Summary ... 23

2.1. Italy, Sardinia, and elsewhere in the Romania
    a. *punga* ... 23
    b. *bracile* ... 27

2.2. Summary ... 28

3.1. Italy and another restricted area of the Romania
    a. *statio* ... 28
    b. *sagellum* ... 30
    c. *taedium* ... 31

3.2. Summary ... 32

4.1. Northern and Central Italy, and Western Romance
    a. *mansionarius* ... 33
    b. *notarius* ... 35
    c. *potestas* ... 37

4.2. Summary ... 39

5.1. Widespread in Italy, and in Romance
    a. *soca* ... 40
    b. *spatharius* ... 43
    c. *testimonium* ... 44
    d. *sarica* ... 47

5.2. Summary ... 49

			Page
D.	Groups of semantically related items with characteristic distribution in Italy		50
	1.1.	Vessels and containers	50
	1.2.	Small	
		a. *caccabellus*	51
		b. *cucumella*	52
	1.3.	Large	
		c. *buttis*	52
		d. *butticella*	53
		e. *tina*	53
		f. *cuppus*	54
	1.4.	Summary	56
	2.1.	Fields	
		a. *campus*	58
		b. *terra*	58
	2.2.	Sown	
		c. *ager*	59
		d. *arvus*	61
		e. *sationalis*	62
	2.3.	Deserted	
		f. *desertus*	63
		g. *incultus*	63
	2.4.	Vineyard	
		h. *vineatus*	64
	2.5.	Summary	65
	3.1.	Dwellings and landed estates	66
	3.2.	House	
		a. *casa*	66
		b. *domus*	67
		c. *domucella*	67
	3.3.	Farmhouse	
		d. *colonica*	68
		e. *casalis*	69
	3.4.	Estate	
		f. *fundus*	71
		g. *praedium*	72
		h. *colonia*	72
		i. *massa*	73
	3.5.	Summary	75
	4.	Church: *ecclesia, basilica*	76
	5.	Day: *dies, feria*	77
E.	Conclusions		82
BIBLIOGRAPHY			97

BRIEF NOTE CONCERNING THE CORPUS

While Tjäder's first volume presumably concerns 28 texts written mainly at Ravenna, Italy, we were obliged in our study to note the following differentiations. Concerning the number of texts the total was first revised downward a) by counting certain pairs of texts whose identifying numbers are linked by a hyphen as one document, and b) by omitting certain texts which were very imperfectly preserved in their entirety (documents 9, 12, 26, 27), and finally upward c) by distinguishing among the various wills (designated as W) and the last portion (designated Concluding Portion) of doc. 4-5, thus giving ultimately a total of 24 separate texts. With regard to place of origin, four texts are not from Ravenna (designated as NR): 7 (Rieti), 10-11 (Syracuse), and 17 and 18-19 (Rome). (Furthermore, doc. 3 is only presumed to be from Ravenna.)

The subject matter of the entire collection is legalistic and may be classified as: texts referring to imperial and royal administration (docs. 1, 2, 3), wills and testaments (4-5, 6), appointment of a guardian (NR-7), a receipt (8), and donations (NR-10-11, 13, 14-15, 16, NR-17, NR-18-19, 20, 21, 22, 23, 24, 25, 28). Thus the content is quite akin to that found in other governmental and ecclesiastical records extant from the Late Latin period. As such they may naturally be expected to confront us with certain linguistic limitations, especially in the use of many fixed formularies. It may further be observed that while the collection spans a period of 255 years, and while the 6th and 7th centuries are quite evenly represented with regard to the total number of texts, it is the category of donations to the Church which completely prevails in the 7th century. Finally we note that many of the documents, donations especially (and also docs. 6 and 8), consist of two distinct portions: the *main body* of the text, written generally by official scribes who appear to be attempting to write according to a Classical Latin norm, and *signatures* of witnesses making depositions, in which a far greater divergence from the orthographical standards of CL is apparent.

It will be apparent in the conclusions drawn from our study that these factors play a role of considerable importance.

STUDIES IN ROMANCE LEXICOLOGY

A. INTRODUCTION

Our study of the lexicon of a collection of documents composed at Ravenna, Italy, between the years AD 445 and 700, emphasizes the history and development of various items from the standpoint of the Romance languages. Instead of dealing with all of the approximately 1200 different lexical forms in the collection, we discuss a group selected according to the following criterion: survival in Romance, with major emphasis placed on forms found in Italy.

The items have been divided into three groups: 1) those which represent etyma which have been in some way noted as uncertain for various Romance forms, 2) single items which are of interest with regard to their semantic evolution and ultimate geographical distribution in the Romania, and 3) groups of items which share a semantic identity and which find a characteristic distribution in Italy today. It will be noted that a major point of differentiation between points 2 and 3 lies in the varying degrees of emphasis as to geographical delimitation. The interest of the third group, which consists of classical and non-CL forms, is Italy. The second series of items consists largely of forms which are non-CL in form or meaning; as for geographical distribution, they often occur not only in Italy but also in other regions of the Romania. Since most of our texts originate in NE Italy, i. e., Ravenna, we treat our items in order of their appearance, first in the north, and then in central and southern Italy; we then proceed elsewhere within the Romania, commencing with restricted locales (e. g., Sardinia), progressing to more generalized areas (e. g., Western Romania).

In passing we point out instances in which our collection represents the first (or almost first) attestation of an item; we include under this rubric words which may have been attested once before (e. g., *tina*, see page 53). As for the phonology of the items, we largely ignore such considerations as the problems have been adequately dealt with earlier. As for date of survival in Romance, most of the items considered occur today; however we have included others which, while no longer extant in a given sense, are no less valid since they appeared in earlier Romance (e. g., *armarium*, see page 17). We also point out that there is overlapping possible in our assignment of an item to the second or third grouping; we have placed such items (e. g., *cuppus*) in the more generally appropriate grouping. Finally, in anticipation of our conclusions, we note the overwhelming importance of one text, doc. 8, written in Ravenna, dated 564, see pages 83ff.

B. Starred items and *capsicius*

The following items have been designated with an asterisk by various Romance scholars: *sarica* (*REW*, *DEI*, Prati, Rohlfs), *caccabellus* (*REW*, Gröber), and *bracile* (Puşcariu). We treat these items more fully in the individual discussions below, see pages 47, 51, 27.

The item *capsicius* (*-ium?*) is of considerable importance in that it represents the etymon of Fr. *châssis* 'window-frame', a fact which has been only alluded to in the literature. The item is found in doc. 8 (Ravenna, 564); since it appears as *capsicio*, absolute determination of its gender is not possible. Tjäder, 511, marks it as *capsicium* (?). It is entirely possible of course that the intended base form should be a masculine form, since it is accompanied by *valente*. On the other hand, *valente* as well as the plural *valentes* appear in our collection as forms referring to any gender; furthermore, note below the form suggested by Gamillscheg.

The form is a derivative of CL *capsa* 'box, case', cf Körting, *Etym. Wörterb.*, 91b. While various suffixes, *-icius, -ile, -inus,* have played a role in the development of various derivatives of this word in Gallo-Roman, it is the first which prevailed to give old Fr. *chassiz,* and old Prov. *chassis,* cf *FEW,* 2, 311a, and 314b. The chronology of derivatives arising from the various processes of suffixation is as follows: *chassiz* 'frame of a rectangular opening—window, door, pane' is attested in *Eneas* (ca. 1150), cf Godefroy, 9, 24c; Tobler-Lommatzsch, 2, 301; *le Roman de Troie* (1165-1170), cf *FEW,* 2, 311a; and subsequently in 1332, 1433, 1488, cf Godefroy. Variant forms with the ending *-ich* are noted for Picard in 1425-1426, 1481, 1542, cf Godefroy, and also Gamillscheg, *Etym.*, 211, who cites the 15th c. In addition, rival forms with a suffix *-il* appear in the 13th c., and in 1372, cf Godefroy, *FEW,* 2, 311b, and Gamillscheg, *Etym.* Such forms doubtless arise from the fact that the suffix *-il(e)* itself has a connotation of "frame". Furthermore, it is most probable that the differentiation between the forms in *-iz* and *-il* is purely one of spelling, inasmuch as the final consonants in both instances were not pronounced. Finally, *cassin* is attested for old Fr. (1324), cf *FEW,* 2, 311b, and doubtless also slightly earlier (1313, 1320), cf Godefroy, 1, 792b, who marks the sense of the former as uncertain, but who in 2, 84b gives the sense '*châssis*'. As we have indicated, only *châssis* survives. The value of doc. 8 lies in its attestation of *capsicio,* which must correspond to the hypothetical etymon *capsiceum proposed by Gamillscheg.

As for the exact sense of the item in our collection, Tjäder's gloss of 'small chest', 243, is doubtless correct owing to the arrangement of items peculiar to doc. 8, in which we find a tendency toward grouping words of closely related meanings *(arca-arcella, satarium-cos,* and many more). *Capsicio* occurs in such a group which deals with containers of one type or another *(panarium, urceolus, olla).* The semantic evolution from 'small chest' doubtless arises from the association of the suffix *-il* (or its phonologically equivalent *-iz*) with the notion of 'frame', cf *FEW,* 2, 314b.

C. Single items restricted in distribution in the Romania

1.1. Italy

a. *runcilio*

Runcilio is a LL item which is to be derived from a CL root *runc-* (e. g., *runco, -onis* 'weeding hook', *runco* 'root up', cf Facciolati-Forcellini, 4, 172c). It appears as *runcilione* in doc. 8 (Ravenna, 564); it is glossed by Tjäder, 434, as 'scythe' or 'gardener's cutting knife'. It is more likely the latter; note the illustrations of other implements of viticulture commencing with *ronc-* in Scheuermeier, 151. *Runcilione* contrasts with *falx (falce missuria)* 'harvest sickle' and the hapax *satario* 'harvest scythe', both of which also appear in doc. 8.

The form *runcilio* (or *runculeu*) appears in Greek-Latin glosses of the *CGL* as follows: 2, 262, 43 (Lyons, 9th c.), 3, 23, 38 (Leyden, 10th c.), and 3, 299, 70 and 71 (Montepessulana, 9th c.). As will be subsequently indicated, however, it is problematical whether such forms and ours are the same. Attestations of *roncilione, runciglione* 'hedgebill' in the Latin of Italy are cited by Sella as follows: near Rome (C. It., 1057), *GLI*, 488; also *DEI*, 5, 3280b; Modena (Emilia, N. It., 1327), *GLE*, 300; and Viterbo (C. It., 1356), *GLI*, 493. The only extant use of the term is in the placename *Ronciglione* (Latium, C. It.).

The item is of interest because of its external similarity to two other main groups of forms, those in *-alis* and those in *-ilio*, modern *-iglio*. The former, so frequent in Du Cange, 7, 238c, however appear in such a different sense, '*ager incultus*', that the connection with *runcilio*, etc., is highly improbable. See also Niermeyer, 10, 924a, who gives *runcalis* 'cleared' from *runcus*. Indeed, the many derivatives found in the Romania, such as *Roncesvalles*, etc., are doubtless to be derived from a CL *rumex* (Fr. *ronce*), cf d'Ovidio, *AGI*, 13, 402f, as well as Körting, *Etym. Wörterb.*, 347a. The second group concerns the forerunner of old and mod. It *ronciglio* 'hook', cited in *REW*, 7444, *DEI*, 5, 3280, and Olivieri, 598a. Although the exact process of derivation is not clear, Meyer-Lübke, *REW*, 7444, suggests a hypothetical intermediary step: *runcile—→ runcilio (compare *CGL* above) → ronciglio. We would then have here merely an instance of affixation of -*ilis*, -*ile* (compare *bracile*, page 27), a rival of -*alis*, -*ale*. Though such suffixes are normally associated with adjectival formation, they serve on occasion to form nouns (compare *casalis*, page 69), cf Grandgent, *Vulg. Lat.*, 23; Stolz-Schmalz, 235-236; Rohlfs, *Hist. Gramm.*, 3, 291. Other derivations also suggest themselves. In the article cited, d'Ovidio suggests as an intermediary step not only *runcile, but also hypothetical forms in -*illus* or -*ellus*. (Olivieri, 598a, merely notes a derivation from *ronca, roncola*, in turn to be derived from CL *runcare*.) With reference to S. Italy and Sardinia, it is the -*illus*, -*ellus* forms which have prevailed; cf *AIS* 542 (P. 707, 722, 728, 791, 824, 826, 851, and 990).

Thus we note a large number of formally similar items but which enjoy different origins or which maintain distinct histories of suffixation. Two further such instances are *runcilus* (Essex, indeterminate date), cited in Du Cange, 5, 826a, and *runcilio* (Lucca, indeterminate date), in Arnaldi. However, the former is equated with *runcalis*, while the latter appears as an abl., and hence presupposes a base *runcilius*, or -*ium*.

In conclusion it is very apparent that no modern Italian word may be derived from *runcilione*. It survives only as a toponomastic term.

b. *armarium*

Armarium is noteworthy for the fact that it demonstrates in our collection a semantic evolution from the CL sense of 'closet', doc. 8 (Ravenna, 564), to 'archive or library', doc. 22 (Ravenna, 639). It is thus observed that doc. 8, which otherwise furnishes a preponderance of our lexical citations, is conservative at this point. Furthermore, the latter sense does not survive into modern Romance; compare It. *armadio*, Fr. *armoire* 'clothes-closet', etc. (the latter likely from *armoria, in turn from *armarium*, cf Körting, *Etym. Wörterb.*, 23a).

However, the sense is attested in a specialized way in N. Italy, Tuscany and Umbria in the 14th c., as '*archivio comunale*', i. e., town record office, cf *DEI*, 1, 291b. We have noted above the apparent inexactitude with regard to the translation given by Tjäder, 470. The meaning of 'library' is noted early, in Tertullian (died ca. 215), cf Du Cange, 1, 389c (with reference to *armaria*), and Blaise, 97b; in an interpretation of Juvenal (composed in the 4th c.), cf Du Cange, and *ThesLL*, 2, 604, 10; and in St. Augustine (354-430), cf Blaise. (For a general attestation of the sense of 'library' in medieval Latin, cf Strecker, 48ff.) Such attestations obviously long antedate our text of the 7th c., though the same sense appears frequently, especially in Belgium, France, Germany and Switzerland, between the 8th and 13th centuries, as in Alcuin (Tours, ca. 773-804), Heito (Reichenau and Basel, 824), Agobardus (Lyons, ca. 816-840), Meginhardus (Fulda, Germany, ca. 825-888), Ekkehardus (St. Gallen, Switzerland, ca. 980-ca. 1060), Lambertus (Deutz, Germany, and Liege, Belgium, before 1070), Wibald (Stavelot, Belgium, as well as Cassino, Italy, and Corbie, France, 1119-1157), Moses Panormitanus (Palermo, ca. 1277), Albertus Magnus (Regensburg and Cologne, Germany, ca. 1270-1280), cf *Mittellat. Wörterb.*, 1:6, 960. (For *armaria* 'library', cf the same source, 1:6, 959.) It is in citations concentrated largely in the 9th c. that the term appears in contexts which relate it to the archives of the palace, etc. In the following outline of attestations, Niermeyer, for example, notes only the sense 'archive' (cf 60b), while in the *Mittellat. Wörterb.* a distinction is made between 'library' and 'archive', both being however treated under the overall heading of place of keeping or preservation of written material: documents pertaining to the Frankish kings (ca. 507-877), a document from Mainz (Germany, 9th c.), documents from Le Mans (France, ca. 9th c.), cf *Mittellat. Wörterb.*, 1:6, 960; Pope Ludovicus (816-817), cf Niermeyer, 60b, and Du Cange, 1, 389c; Council of Paris (825), Pope Ludovicus (ca. 835), Charles the Bald (France, 840-877), cf Niermeyer; documents from Thurgau (Switzerland, 724-1280), and documents from Westphalia (Germany, 809-1280), cf *Mittellat. Wörterb.* The first instance which we find, apart from earlier references to the Roman pope, of localization of the term in Italy is in Ferrara (Emilia, N. It., 840), cf Tjäder, 470. We mention in passing only a doubtful instance of the use in the *liber pontificalis* of Pope Zacharias (741-752, life composed by Anastasius, 800-879), cf Du Cange, 1, 389c. The interchangeability of *armarium* with other forms is dramatically illustrated in the following citation, which is written by the Saxon Aelfric (died 1006): *bibliotheca, vel armarium vel archivum,* cf Du Cange, 1, 389c. Compare the much later *Glosario de Toledo* 588, *biblioteca, -e: armario* (late 14th c.-early 15th c.), cf Castro, 18, 176, 318. Similarly, Hakamies, 10b, gives the sense 'bibliothèque, archives' in a text written in Finland (1363).

It is apparent that the attestations which appear after doc. 22 (639) are concentrated largely in the space of two centuries. Geographically they originate at fairly diverse points of the Latin speaking world. Nonetheless most of the citations are from C. and N. Italy. Very likely the occurrences cited for Rome and N. Italy (our collection and also the citation from Ferrara) are precursors of the 14th c. use in what is approximately the same regions.

Finally we note *scrinium* which occurs in docs. 2 (Ravenna, 565-570) and 22 (as above); in the latter document it is associated with *armarium*. It is significant in that it undergoes a parallel semantic development, from CL 'box or chest for keeping papers' to 'department, bureau, government office'. We do not further treat it in detail inasmuch as it is not attested later in Romance in the extended sense.

c. *necessus*

Non-CL *necessus* occurs in doc. 17 (Rome, beginning of the 7th c.?). It occurs with *necesse* and *necessarius* in highly comparable contexts: *cum necesse fuerit* (8-1-7), and *si necessarium fuerit* (13-46). *Necessus* (or *-um*) is well attested in the literature. In Ernout-Meillet, *Dict. étym.*, 434b, and Stolz-Schmalz, 640, the *-um* form is considered the result of analogical influence exerted by *aequum;* Ernout-Meillet further cite the influence of *opus* on *necessus. Necessus* may also be considered an archaising form; it is cited early as follows: Scipio (3rd c. BC), the *senatusconsultus* concerning the *Bacchanales* (186 BC), Terence (died 159 BC), cf Walde-Hofmann, 152-153; Lucretius (died 55 BC), cf Walde-Hofmann, and Ernout-Meillet, 434-435; Cornificus (born ca. AD 95), cf Ernout-Meillet; and Aulus Gellius (died AD 175), cf Walde-

Hofmann, and Ernout-Meillet. For more on *necessarius, necesse, -um,* cf also Muller, 284f.

Dialectally, reflexes of *necessus, -um* are found in old Ven., old Lomb. *(necesso),* and old Sic. *(necessu)* cf *REW,* 5871, and *DEI,* 4, 2560a. With reference to the old Lomb. form, cf Salvioni, *AGI,* 12, 416, who derives the examples from the following sources: *"Antica Parafrasi lombarda del 'Neminem laedi nisi a se ipso' di S. Giovanni Grisostomo"*, edited by Foerster, *AGI,* 7 (no *locus* is given); and *"Antiche scritture lombarde"*, *AGI,* 9, 22, 17. (Neither is further identified as to date; the latter is from Como.)

We mention briefly also dialectal reflexes which are apparently from CL *necesse. REW,* 5871, and *DEI,* 4, 2560a, both cite old It. *necesse* and especially Friul. *nisise.* Since *necesse* appears in Dante, it is very likely merely a Latinism. As for the Friulan form, however, great uncertainty prevails as to its status as an adjective or a noun. Ascoli, who was first to discuss the form, obviously treated it as a noun, and derived it thus: *niçisse* ← * *necésta* (or * *necestas*) ← *necessità,* cf *AGl,* 2, 437, and 3,260. Giacomino, *AGl,* 15, 429, similarly considered it a noun. Unfortunately, we have been provided with no context so as to be better able to judge; nonetheless the fact remains that the later commentators, Körting, *Lat.-Rom. Wörterb.*, 686, *REW,* and *DEI,* classed the item (spelled variously *nisiss, nisise,* and derived by Körting from *necesse*) as an adjective. On the basis of the evidence available, this action seems unwarranted. Furthermore, *REW,* 5871, and *DEI,* 4, 2560a, class under one rubric all of the forms in question here, the reflexes of *necessus (-um)* as well as the old It. *necesse* and the questionable Friul. form, without consideration of the evident dual etyma.

In addition to *necessum* (doc. 17, Rome), the item *necessae* (for *necesse)* appears in 10-11 (Syracuse, 489), as well as in 1 and 8 (both Ravenna). Hence it appears that our collection offers one contradiction, and possibly two: 1) the reflexes of *necessus (-um)* are attested dialectally for N. and S. Italy, whereas doc. 17 is from Rome; and 2) doc. 10-11 is from Syracuse, while the reflex of CL *necesse* is possibly attested in Friulan.

d. *horticellus*

Horticellus or *orticellus*, mod. It. *orticello*, finds its first attestation in our collection, where it appears in docs. 21 (Ravenna, 625) and 25 (Ravenna, 1st half of the 7th c.). The form is obviously a diminutive derivation from CL *hortus*, and serves in place of CL *hortulus*; it is noteworthy for the fact that it survives only in Italian. Compare our discussions of *vineatus*, page 64, and *domucella*, page 67.

Cooper, 185, considered the ending *-cello*, with reference to *orticello*, to be a development of Italian. After our citations from the 7th c., the following are noted: Pope Stephen III (also known as Stephen II) (755), cf Niermeyer, 499b, and Du Cange, 4, 235c; Lucca (C. It., 9th-10th c.), cf Arnaldi; Tivoli (Latium, C. It., 954), cf Sella, *GLI*, 393; Ravenna (957), cf Sella, *GLE*, 240; Rome (959), cf Arnaldi. It is apparent that the attestations thus far are somewhat more heavily weighted in favor of Central Italy. In the 11th century, the balance shifts to the north: Rimini (S. Emilia, 1073), cf Sella, *GLE*, 240; Ravenna (11th c.), cf Arnaldi. The early and late predominance of Emilian attestations, coupled with the positive localization in Ravenna in four of the instances, makes it highly probable that the item originated in Ravenna and spread from there into C. Italy, and ultimately into standard Italian. (We note the presence of additional later citations for Ravenna in the following work cited by Tjäder, 466: M. Fantuzzi, *Monumenti ravennati de'secoli di mezzo per la maggior parte inediti*, Venice, 1801-1804.

e. *cata*

Cata is a direct borrowing of the Greek preposition κατά. It is widespread in the Romance languages, but almost always in indefinite pronominal formations, cf *FEW*, 2, 482b, for such developments. In doc. 6 (Ravenna, 575), it conserves a local sense, and is equated with CL *penes* 'in the power or in the presence of', cf Tjäder, 422. The form is well attested in the literature as an equivalent of such prepositions designating place as *iuxta*, *secundum*, or *per*. The following citations occur in *ThesLL*, 3, 585, 52ff, Stolz-Schmalz, 522-523, or in Blaise, 137b: *Itala* (2nd or 3rd c.), St. Cyprianus (Carthaginian, before 257), *Peregrinatio* (possibly Spanish, probably 383), and St. Filastrius (bishop of Brescia, Lombardy, before 397). As an equivalent specifically of *penes*, the item is found in documents which are more coincident with the time of our text, i. e., the 6th c.: *Novellae* of Justinian (6th c.), cf *ThesLL*, 3, 585, 66; Stolz-Schmalz; and Souter, 41b; *Oribasius* (a doctor from Asia Minor, 325-403; however the work named after him is 6th c.), cf Arnaldi; and various Christian inscriptions (7th c.), cf *ThesLL*, Stolz-Schmalz, and Souter. Attestations from sources posterior to our text are frequent in medieval Latin and occur in diverse areas: Pope Stephanus II (8th c.), Anastasius (9th c.), Pope Leo III (9th c.), S. Willibaldus (bishop of Eichstätt, Franconia; 700-ca. 781), etc., cf Du Cange, 2, 216a. It is apparent that we can claim neither a first attestation for our text, or trace any correlation between Ravenna and the uses cited here.

On the contrary, the form appears dialectally in modern Italian, where it is heavily concentrated in the south. It is commonly linked with another preposition, generally *ad*, occasionally *in*. The following locales are noted in the *AIS* 705 'at the doctor's': S. Abr. (P. 668), Apul. (P. 706, 707, 708, 709), Basilic. (P. 726), Camp. (P. 712, 720), and Calab. (P. 751); additional points in 1637 'have him come to our place': Basilic. (P. 726, 733), Camp. (P. 715), Calab. (P. 772, 780, 783, 794). (*AIS* 1585 'in the store' adds no new points.) The same situation is further noted in the south by Rohlfs in the following works: *Arch. Rom.*, 7, 461 ('in the house', Campania, Apulia), *Hist. Gramm.* 3, 90f ('at my place' or 'at our place', S. Abruzzi, Apulia), and *Diz. dial.*, 2, 78 (Calabria). Finally the item appears as a formative in toponomastic terms in Campobasso (Molise, S. It.); place names beginning with *Cata-* originate from prior use of the preposition to indicate direction toward a place, cf de Bartholomaeis, *AGl*, 15, 336.

In conclusion, we may regard the occurrence of *cata* in our collection as having no more bearing on modern dialectal distribution than any of the other early attestations, not one of which was identifiable as southern.

1.2. Summary

Of the five forms presented above, two, *runcilio* and *horticellus*, are found first in our collection. The former, however, is found today only as a place-name in C. Italy. As for the other items, *horticellus* is attested today in standard Italian, whereas *necessus* (*-um*) and *cata* appear only dialectally. With regard to these two items, the evidence of our texts is quite contrary to what we actually find in the way of geographical distribution inasmuch as the south is especially favored today. Our collection demonstrates that such items which now appear in a very conservative part of the Romania were more widely distributed at an earlier time. *Armarium* persists into standard Italian, however not in the sense found in our texts which reaches its peak of semantic evolution in the 12th century in N. and C. Italy. Items for which we find a partial correlation between the area of our texts and the regions in which the items are attested in medieval Latin are *armarium*, *horticellus*, and *runcilio*, all of which are situated in N. and C. Italy. In short, the last three items seemingly show a possible direct connection between our texts and the development in Italy; however only one form persists in modern times in the appropriate sense. In contrast, *cata* and *necessus* both survive but are far removed from the regions in which our texts originated; only an indirect connection is inferred.

2.1. Italy, Sardinia, and Elsewhere in the Romania

a. *punga*

In *punga* we have an instance of a form whose origin is disputed. On the basis of our earlier research it was our belief that the form was of Gothic origin, but that it entered LL either directly from a Gothic source or else via the intermediary of Greek. As a matter of fact, it enjoys a high degree of attestation in both the Germanic and Romance languages, as well as in a variety of other languages. Although the Gothic nominative is hypothetical (*puggs), an accusative *pugg* is noted by Feist, *Etym. Wörterb.*, 290a, and *Vergl.*

Wörterb., 385a. Various derivatives and related forms are cited in Germanic (old Icel., old Eng., OHG, MHG, old Norse, old Dutch, Swedish, and Danish), cf Feist, Diefenbach, vol. 1, 338, de Cihac, 299, Schulze, 140b, Skeat, 453b. The occurrence of the item or of related forms is further observed in such non-Romance languages as Cyprian, Greek, Keltic, Albanian, Estonian, etc., cf Schulze, de Cihac, Skeat, *Lesicon Románescu*, 560a, Diefenbach. In E. Romania it appears in Rum. *pungă* 'money purse', cf *REW*, 6849; *DEI*, 4,3014a; Gamillscheg, *Rom. Germ.*, 252-253; Diefenbach; Barcianu, 209b. Conjectures as to which of these languages we may attribute the original form are various: apart from Gothic or Greek, which most of our sources point to as the language of origin, certain commentators have suggested old Slavic (Miklosich, cited by Diefenbach, vol. 2, 756, with reference to the form *puggs*) while Skeat, 453b, considers the related Eng. *poke* to be from Keltic. De Cihac notes merely, 299, that 'l'étymologie du mot est obscure'.

Be this as it may, the immediate etymon of the Romance form offers additional problems with regard to exact form and also to date. Our sources are in general agreement that a form πουγγα or πουγγη existed in middle Greek, cf Feist, *Etym. Wörterb.*, 290a; Rohlfs, "*Germ. Spracherbe*", 22-23; Gamillscheg, *Rom. Germ.*, 252-253; Diefenbach, vol. 1, 338; Schulze, 140b; de Cihac, 299. However these forms are not cited in such pertinent works as Sophocles or Estienne. On the contrary, both Du Cange, 6, 572a, and Sophocles, 913a, cite πουγγίον, which Sophocles declares is "Latinized" into *punga*. Since such a Greek form would produce *pungium in Latin, the question of the Greek form remains. With reference to the date of the presumed "middle" Greek form, Sophocles further notes, 10, that the term "medieval Greek" should be applied only to the second epoch of the Byzantine period, i. e., between 622-1099. As we shall subsequently point out, *punga* is attested in our collection in the 6th century; furthermore we note a usage of a Greek form in Mauricius (607), cf Sophocles, 913a.

Notwithstanding these discrepancies, *punga* is first attested in Latin in doc. 8 (Ravenna, 564). Subsequent occurrences appear over a long period of time and in a relatively large geographical area: the *Vita* of Eligius (France, mid-8th c.), cf Niermeyer, 872b; Du Cange, 6, 572a; Gaeta (Campania, 792-1069), cf de Bartholomaeis, *AGl* 15, 352; Camaldoli (province of Arezzo, Tuscany; 992), cf Arnaldi; Farfa (province of Rieti, Umbria; 1125), cf Sella, *GLI*, 453; *DEI*, 4, 3014a; Hariulfus (Aldenbourg, Germany; ca. 1060-1143), cf Niermeyer, and Du Cange, 6, 572a. (As for the sense of the foregoing, certain of the sources, especially Sella and Arnaldi, give a meaning of 'measure'·, which they qualify as uncertain; Du Cange, 6, 405c, similarly treats of a variant *ponga* 'mensura'·.)

As we shall shortly point out with reference to the possible source of the form in Italy (i. e., directly from Gothic or indirectly via Greek), the most important attestation which we have from the standpoint of old It. is that found in Jacopone da Todi (province of Perugia, in Umbria; 1230-1306) in the sense of 'purse'·, cf *DEI*, 4, 3014a.

In the following dialectal attestations for modern Italy and Sardinia, a seemingly varied complex of meanings appears; however it will be noted that all are related to the idea of a small purse or pad or container of some sort: (North) Ven. 'bird's craw'·, cf *REW*, 6849; *DEI*, 4, 3104a; Feist, *Etym. Wörterb.*, 290b, and *Vergl. Wörterb.*, 385; de Cihac, 299; (Central) Rieti 'small cushion, pad or bolster'·, cf *REW, DEI*; (South) Otranto (in Apulia) 'pocket'·, cf *DEI*; Bova (in Calabria) 'pocket'·, cf *DEI*; and Sardinia (Logud. and Campid.) 'amulet, good-luck charm' (a small purse containing herbs for warding off the evil eye), cf *REW; DES*, 2, 322b.

As we have noted, doc. 8 was composed in Ravenna in 564, merely a few years after the conquest of the city from the Goths by Belisarius on command of the Byzantine emperor Justinian, in 540. Given these dates and the one locale which was occupied by two different cultures, a case may be made either for the Gothic or the Greek source of the word prior to its entry into Latin. In addition, the modern attestations in Venetia and Arezzo lend themselves to either side of the argument; though both are somewhat removed from Ravenna, it is very likely that *punga* could have spread to these points from within the confines either of the Ostrogothic domain or of the Exarchate of Ravenna. However, on the face of it, there appears to be a remarkably high correlation between the remaining attestations and the Byzantine civilization in Italy. Absolute correspondences between modern distribution and the Byzantine settlements are noted for Apulia and Sardinia. However the following objections may be noted: 1) when we are confronted with an attestation from a locale such as Bova, in Calabria, which is an enclave of Greek speech in Italy, there is no way of determining when the form came into use; cf Migliorini, 47, 82, who notes the difficulty of dating Greek forms within the period 476-960, or later; and 2) given the general disinclination on the part of the Goths for writing in their own language we have less possibility of determining whether the form was actively used by them in Italy; cf Miglorini, 46, who notes that even the Arian priests of Ravenna made their signature more frequently in Latin than in Gothic. With these reservations in mind we however note the additional correspondences in the case of the early attestations from Todi (13th c.) and Farfa (12th c.) and the modern citation from Rieti. Strictly speaking, only Todi had been within the area of the Byzantine domain (between the Pentapolis of the E. coast and the duchy of Rome); Farfa and Rieti fall within the confines of the old Lombardic duchy of Spoleto. However, the Lombards and the Byzantines, given their geographical proximity, had been in close contact. Cf Miglorini, 51, who observes that despite a political division of Italy, whereby Byzantium was largely restricted to the south (ca. 680), there was no interruption in the linguistic "circulation" of Byzantium which remained strong in the old Exarchate (including the corridor which we mentioned above along the Via Flaminia, as well as Venetia, Bari, Amalfi, Naples, etc.). Furthermore, after the donation of Ravenna and the Exarchate to Pope Stephen II (756), Byzantine influence, now only in the south, subsequently (early 10th c.) experienced a rebirth of political and cultural force not only in Campania, Apulia, and Calabria, but also in the Lombardic domains (for example, Byzantium occupied Benevento in 891), cf Migliorini, 54; *Diz. encicl. it.*, 2, 199b. Hence the whole question of chronology remains with reference to the various times at which *punga* may have been introduced throughout Italy. The indisputable fact that we have concerning its first appearance in Latin is that it is attested as early as the 6th c. in Ravenna; whether that particular event is to be attributed to the Ostrogoths or the Greeks of that time is not ascertainable.

Finally it is of interest to note that S. Italy attests not only to *punga*, possibly from Gothic but in this case most likely via Greek, but also to a form *poscia* (in Apulia), from a related Frankish form *pokka;* however this was imported by the Normans, cf Rohlfs, "*Germ. Spracherbe*", 22, 35.

b. *bracile*

Bracile is a LL neologism which is however derived from CL *braca(e)* (itself of Keltic origin). Compare our remarks on the processes of derivation in *runcilio* and *casalis,* pages 17, 69. It appears in doc. 8 (Ravenna, 564), which is roughly contemporaneous with the following citations: Isidore, XIX, xxxiii, 5 (Spain; 570-ca. 640), cf Blaise, 118b; Forcellini, 1, 580b; *CGL,* 5, 412, 35; Du Cange, 1, 731b; *FEW,* 1, 482b; the Benedictine *regula* (6th c.), cf *CGL,* Du Cange, Forcellini; the Salic Law (end of the 6th c.), cf Du Cange, *FEW;* the *Vita* of St. Germanus (written by Venantius Fortunatus, bishop of Poitiers; 530-ca. 605), cf Du Cange, 1, 731b; Fredegarius (possibly from Burgundy, lst half of the 7th c.), cf Blaise, 118b. Other attestations are from a considerably later period: St. Hildegard (Bingen, Germany; ca. 1100-ca. 1179), Joanne de Janua (Genoa, died 1286), a history of the Albigensians (13th c. or later), cf Du Cange. Sleumer, 171b, associates *bracile, -is* 'girdle to a monk's habit' specifically with Christian Latin.

In older stages of Romance, *brakile* is attested in Sardinia (old Logud.), cf *REW,* 1258; *DEI,* 1, 581b. With regard to Gaul, however, there is little doubt that, despite the numerous citations above, forms cited in Godefroy, *braiel, brael, brahel, brail, breil,* 'belt', do not come from our form. We further point out our disagreement with *FEW,* 1, 479b, which gives *-ile* as the origin of the old Fr. forms. The question (which is somewhat analogous to that already treated in *runcilio,* see page 17) involves the matter of different suffixes, *-alis* or *-ilis,* as well as *-ellus.* We note further that despite the fact that Godefroy has grouped all such forms together in his heading, none of his examples actually shows *brail* (from *bracile*). Similarly, *brael* and *braiel,* but not *brail,* are cited in Tobler-Lommatzsch, 1, 1112. Thus the same question of a possible reflex in old Swiss French *braye* is purely hypothetical. The form is cited as a possible reflex of an old Fr. form *braiel* (presumably ← * *bracellus*), cf *Gloss. des pat. de la SR,* fasc. 23, 748a; however since we have shown that the old Fr. form is not pertinent to our word, then we reject any possible continuation in Swiss French.

On the other hand, in addition to old Sard., the only survival of our item occurs in Rum. brăciri, given uniformly in the sources as a reflex of bracile, cf REW, 1258; DEI, 1, 581b; Puşcariu, 18 (who erroneously marks it with an asterisk), and Cioranescu, 101. The change in intervocalic $l \rightarrow r$ is typical to Rumanian, cf Bourciez, 525.

Thus *bracile* is later attested in two very conservative regions of the Romania. Coupled with the fact that we find the item first in Ravenna, the later attestations in conservative areas bespeak an earlier distribution which was certainly far more widespread.

2.2. SUMMARY

Although they have totally dissimilar origins, *punga* and *bracile* share several important characteristics, in terms of first (or nearly first) attestation in Italy, a history of attestation in medieval Latin, and finally their distribution in the Romania. Although *bracile* is no longer found in Sardinian, both items have occurred there as well as in Rumanian, two highly conservative linguistic communities within the Romania. The matter of reflexes of *bracile* in old Fr. or modern Swiss French dialects is highly doubtful. Finally, *punga* is perhaps the best example in our collection of a form for which many of the medieval attestations seemingly correlate well with the findings of modern dialect geography.

3.1. ITALY AND ANOTHER RESTRICTED AREA OF THE ROMANIA

a. *statio*

Statio, -onem, a CL item which originally meant 'a state of standing still', later undergoes considerable semantic extension ('place of abode', 'station of the Cross', etc.). It is applied in the following contexts to various places of business: (doc. 6, Ravenna, 575) *Iulianus... scribtor... et adiutor Iohannis forensis, habens stationem apud sanctum Iohannem Baptista* (28-29), and *Quiria-*

cus... orrearius, qui tenet stationem ad domo Otratarit (42); (doc. 18-19, Rome, beginning of the 7th c. ?) *Theodosius... tabellio urbis Romae, habens stationem in porticum de Subora* (59-60). It is apparent that *statio* encompasses a variety of businesses, from presumably a booth or stand on a square to the business place of a warehouse manager. With specific reference to the use of *statio* as applied to *tabelliones* who plied their skills in the Forum in Rome, cf *Enc. catt.*, 8, cols. 1955-59, and *RE*, 2nd series, 4, 1849a. (Note its connection in our text from Ravenna with *scriptor* as well.) For our current purposes, we treat the item in its most general sense of place of business, and follow its evolution to the restrictive sense of 'store, shop'.

Attestations which antedate both of our texts appear in Fulgentius (born in Africa, lived in Sicily and Rome; died 532) 'shop', cf Du Cange, 7, 587a; Cassiodorus (born in Bruttium, mod. Calabria; ca. 480 - ca. 580), 'merchant's stand or booth at a fair', cf Blaise, 774a; Souter, 387a; the *Novellae, Codex* and *Digesta* of Justinian (mid-6th c.), 'merchant's stall or booth', cf Mohrmann, 227; Heumann-Seckel, 553; *RE*, 2nd series, 4, 1849a. At a considerably later date, commencing in the 10th century, we find an extremely heavy concentration of attestations of *statio "bottega'* for N. Italy, in particular in Emilia and Venetia. In the following listing, taken generally from Sella and Du Cange, the only two exceptions are citations from Rome (citations not marked as being from Venetia are to be classed with Emilia): Ravenna (10th c.), Imola *(stazone)* (1194), Verona (Venetia, 1206), cf Du Cange, 7,587a; Bologna (1245), and Parma (1255), cf *GLE*, 130, 340, 323; Rome (13th c.), Padua (Venetia, 13th c.), cf *GLI*, 350, 530; Piacenza (13th c.), Bologna (13th c.), cf *GLE*, 13, 39; Vicenza (Venetia, 1264), cf *GLI*, 428; (Padua, 1272), cf Du Cange, 7, 587a; Parma (14th c.), cf *GLE*, 3, 13, 87, 313, 340; Verona (1319), *GLI*, 41, 151, 276; Modena (1327), cf *GLE*, 309; Ragusa (1356), cf *GLI*, 546; Cremona (1387), cf Bosshard, 192; Bobbio (1388), cf *GLE*, 80; Parma (15th c.), cf *GLE*, 288; Verona (1450), and Bassano (Venetia, 1506), cf *GLI*, 246, 82.

This overwhelming concentration in the northeast is further confirmed by old Ven. *staço (< statio)* 'shop, store', cf *REW*, 8234; *stazzone* is also attested in old It. (13th c.) as 'shop', cf *REW, DEI*, 5, 3623b, and Olivieri, 664a (*'bottega di mercante'*). It is thus seen that the medieval Latin and the old It. forms, which are roughly contemporaneous, have the same sense. With regard to modern dialectal attestations, we see that the modern reflexes of *statio, -onem* no longer occur in Emilia or Venetia, but are to be found in very conservative neighboring areas of Romance. Most of the citations concern W. Rheto-Romance, as *stizzum* 'business', cf *DEI*, 5, 3623b; *AIS* 1585 'shop' (P. 5, 13, 15, 16), and especially Sursilvan *štitsun*, etc. 'store', cf *REW*, 8234; *AIS*, 1585 (P. 1, 3, 10, 11). A derivative *Stazzona* occurs as a place-name on Lake Como (Lombardy), cf Olivieri, 664a. Finally, *stasaun* is cited for Vegliote, cf *REW*, and also Bartoli, in *Jagić-Fest.*, 45, who notes that derivatives of *stationem* '*bottega*' are found in Serbo-Croatian and Slovenian, having been carried into the Balkans by Italian commercial travelers of the middle ages.

It is apparent that there exists an unbroken tradition in Italy of use of the term, now in the sense of place of business, now as a specific shop or store; although the sense is attested long before the time of our texts, it is evident that it is later perpetuated and preserved in the north. In its present occurrences it is found however restricted to some of the most remote regions of the Romania. Unlike *punga*, which was found to be a word imported from outside the Romania, *statio* is an "export" in such areas as the Balkans.

b. *sagellum*

Sagellum, which appears in doc. 8 (Ravenna, 564), is a LL diminutive formation of CL *sagum* 'coarse woollen blanket or mantle'. It appears in place of CL *sagulum* 'small military cloak'. The exact signification of the item varies in our sources: 'travelling coat', cf Tjäder, 243; '*petit manteau ou couverture*', cf Blaise, 733a; '*coperta*', cf Arnaldi, Sella, *GLE*, 302 (concerning a parallel masc. form, *sagellus: stragulum lecti*); 'a little *sagum*', cf Souter, 361b. With regard to our collection, Tjäder's translation is most appropriate for the following reasons: 1) the non-CL form *scamnile* already is employed in the sense of 'cover' in doc. 8, and 2) *sagello* appears immediately after *lena* (< *laena*) and hence follows the general pattern in the text whereby items of similar sense are most generally grouped together. See page 15. In the following citations, however, we shall not differentiate among the various senses possible.

The form is first attested in Cassianus (a monk who travelled in the Orient, and thence to Marseilles; ca. 360-435), cf Blaise, 733a, Souter, 361b. Contemporaneous with our document 8 (564) is an occurrence in the *Vitae patrum Iurensium* (Jura, 6th c.), cf Blaise, and Niermeyer, 929a. Subsequent occurrences appear in Alcuin (ca. 773-804); an unidentifiable work of 808; in St. Gallen (Switzerland, 816); and a *Vita* of Eugendus (otherwise not identified as to place or era), cf Niermeyer, 929a; and Longobardic Code (905-906), cf Arnaldi. In terms of the later attestation of the form in old Prov., those with a possible connection with France (Cassianus, the Jura, Alcuin) assume great significance. *Sagelh* appears in old Prov. (in Guilhem d'Autpol, 1280) as '*sorte de vêtement*', cf *FEW*, 2, 74b, and Corom., 4, 166b; Raynouard, 5, 131b. We note in passing that, in view of its attestation from as early as ca. 400, *sagellum* merits a separate entry in the *FEW*.

With reference to Italy, *sagellum* appears to leave no trace; its later attestation in S. France however is possibly the result of an unbroken tradition commencing as early as the 4th or 5th c. in the person of Cassianus.

c. *taedium*

In its CL sense, *taedium* meant 'irksomeness, loathsomeness'; it is evident that in the usage of our text (1, Ravenna; 445-446) it had evolved into 'illness'. Comparison of the following texts is pertinent to this development: *detentus tedio* (1-47) and *egritudine detentus* (4-5: 6th W-VII-1; also Ravenna, 552). Note, however, that the relative chronology is not what we might expect; it is the non-CL usage which predates the correct usage by approximately a century.

Our citation in doc. 1 appears to be among the first occurrences of the new sense; however it is preceded by an instance in Marcellus Empiricus (Bordeaux, beginning of the 5th c.), cf Souter, 412b. Others which appear shortly thereafter are: Theodorus Priscianus (4th-5th c. ?), cf Souter; Ruricius (Limoges, 5th c.); Alcimus (also known as Avitus, bishop of Vienne, in the Dauphiné; ca. 450-518); Council of Epaona (exact location unknown, possibly in

Valais, Isère, Drôme, or the Haute-Savoie; 517); Council of Orléans (533); Gregory of Tours (538-594); and Council of Tours (567), cf Blaise, 807b; Souter, 412b; and Du Cange, 8, 12a. A later example is cited from Salerno (Campania; prior to 974), cf Arnaldi.

As was the case in *sagellum*, we find attestation of *taedium* in the sense of 'illness' almost exclusively in Gaul. However our only dialectal evidence in Romance is found in the forms *teyo*, *teo*, which occur far removed from Gaul in Galicia in the specialized sense of 'sheep staggers', cf *REW*, 8522; *DEI*, 5, 3738b; Corom., 4, 410a; and Herzog, *Zeit. f. rom. Phil.*, 27, 126. (Olivieri, 684b, also cites an early Romance *tiegio* in the same sense, but fails to specify a locale.) Since Galicia represents a very conservative part of the Romania, it is conceivable that the modern forms are reflexes of usage of which we have no records; on the basis of our evidence, it appears however highly unlikely that there is any connection between our documents and Galician.

3.2. Summary

In the three items, *statio*, *sagellum*, and *taedium*, we have seen apparent instances of survival in highly restricted locales within the Romania. In the case of *sagellum* only we are dealing with a neologism; the interest of the other two items lies in their semantic development. We have noted, too, that none of the uses appears first in our collection. As for attestation in medieval Latin, *statio* is best accounted for in terms of sheer number of citations. *Statio* is similary our best example for showing a geographical connection between the earlier citation for N. Italy, and the modern situation in the relatively conservative neighboring regions. Both *sagellum* and *taedium* are best attested in the medieval period in Gaul; only in the case of *sagellum* is this possibly of significance, however. The appearance of reflexes of *taedium* in Galician in a sense comparable to that found in our text appears to be largely a chance ocurrence.

4.1. NORTHERN AND CENTRAL ITALY, AND WESTERN ROMANCE

a. *mansionarius*

Mansionarius is a non-CL neologism which is easily accounted for as a derivative of CL *mansio*, via addition of the suffix *-arius*. It is representative of a type of word formation which is frequent in our collection. It is originally attested as an adjectival in the sense 'belonging to a dwelling', as in Fulgentius (born in Africa, lived in Sicily and Rome; died 532), cf *ThesLL*, 8, 3, 326; *FEW*, 6, 254a; *DEI*, 3, 2353b; and Blaise, 514a. The shift in sense to that of "church servant or caretaker' is explicable from the fact that the person involved lived at or near the building, cf *FEW*. In the course of the semantic development of the item, the exact meaning has varied; it has included the notions of church servant, and more specifically that of a sacristan or a sexton, who might or might not be in orders, cf *Enc. catt.*, 7, cols. 1979-1980. In doc. 17 (Rome, beginning of the 7th c. ?), it is glossed by Tjäder, 327, 333, as *'Kirchendiener'* and *'Kirchenwächter'*, i. e., 'servant' or 'watchman', of a church. In Rome the institution of the *mansionarius* is attested from the 6th c. on, cf Cabrol, *Dict. d'arch. chrét.*, 10: 2, cols. 1582-1585; hence the use in our text is doubtless antedated by a short period. Other attestations from this period are: Gregory the Great (540-604), Rusticus (a deacon of the Roman Church; 6th c.), cf variously *ThesLL*, 8, 326, 10; Blaise, 514b; Niermeyer, 640b; Du Cange, 5, 227c; and Grossi-Gondi, 151. Citations which are more nearly coincident with the presumed date of our text are Benedictus II (died 685), John V (died 686), while the following are cited in the next century: Gregory II (died 731), *Ordo Romanus I* (end of the 7th c.), cf Du Cange, 5, 227c, and Niermeyer, 641a. Indeed, the attestations continue very frequent through the 12th c. We refer to further such examples in Niermeyer; *CGL*, 5, 423, 18; Arnaldi; Blaise, 514b; Du Cange, 5, 227c; and Blatt, 139a. As we have noted, however, there is a pronouncedly Roman cast to the citations which we have listed above. This continues in large measure in the later citations, with the general exception of those found in Blatt which are most often localized in Germany, for example, Frising (806), a *Vita* of Chrodegangus (bishop of Metz; composed in the 10th c.), a document from Ratisbonne (1185), etc. This is highly significant in light of the mod. German form *Messner* 'sexton, sacristan', which is derived as follows, from MHG (ca. 12th c.) *mess(e)naere*←late OHG (prior to the 11th c.) *mesinâri, which is itself to be derived from a medieval Latin *mesenarius* ← *mansionarius*. Cf Kluge, 474b; Schade, 605a; and *FEW*, 6, 254a.

This development is of great importance when we are confronted with the question of dialectal reflexes in Italy. In old Lomb., *masenar* (compare the medieval Latin form cited above in the German development) appears in the specific sense of 'secular servant assigned to a convent or living there', cf *REW*, 5312; *DEI*, 3, 2354a; *FEW*, 6, 253b; Salvioni, *AGl*, 12, 413 (who unjustifiably derives the dialectal form from standard Italian *mansionario*). In the far more restrictive sense of 'female servant', the form *mažnera*, etc. persists today in W. Rheto-Romance (Grisons), cf *REW*, 5312; *DEI*, 3, 2354a; *FEW*, 6, 253b; and *AIS* 1593 'she is a good servant' (P. 2, 29). Finally the fact remains that in the various citations which we have alluded to earlier and which we might have adduced for medieval Latin, there are virtually none which show a real connection with Lombardy or Rheto-Romance. Indeed the only example which we have which might in some way support the later northern dialectal forms is a citation from Novalesa in the Piedmont from the 11th c., cf Niermeyer, 641a; Du Cange, 5, 227c. In partial summation, we may conclude that our document is merely corroborative of the many attestations of use of *mansionarius* in Rome. It is of no greater value in establishing a possible link with the dialectal forms of the north than any of the other attestations. Yet the crucial fact remains that, not only do we find a later tradition in the dialects and in German, but the form is indeed quite widely distributed in the Western Romance languages, in various related senses: old Fr. *maisnier* 'servant', cf *REW*, 5312; *DEI*, 3, 2354a; *FEW*, 6, 253b; Olivieri, 592a; Godefroy, 5, 296a, 'a domestic of all types, attached to a house'; old Prov. *maisnier* 'mercenary soldier', cf *REW*, *DEI*, *FEW*; and Sp. *mesonero* 'host', cf *REW*; *DEI*; *FEW*, 6, 254a; Corom., 3, 233a. In these instances, too, we have no corroborative evidence from medieval Latin.

In conclusion, we note that the true continuator of Roman 'church servant' is found in German; related meanings and forms appear in N. Italy and Rhaetia, but we see no visible tie with our collection. As for the various attestations in Western Romance, they are irrelevant for our purposes.

b. *notarius*

Notarius appears in CL as a derivative of *nota* 'mark, sign', via the same process of suffixation noted above for non-CL *mansionarius*. The item undergoes considerable amplification and subsequent specialization in sense, from classical 'short-hand writer' (until the time of Vopiscus, born 305, cf *DEI*, 4, 2602b), to 'secretary' or 'amanuensis', cf *FEW*, 7, 199b; Niermeyer, 721b. Ultimately the form assumes a specialized legal sense, which it enjoys today in certain of the Romance languages (see below), of 'notary public', i. e., one who draws up and authenticates legal acts. For the development of this latter sense, cf Cabrol, *Dict. d'arch. chrét.*, 12:2, cols. 1623-1640. In the broad sense of 'public secretary', *notarius* is found early in competition with such forms as *tabellio* and *scriba*, cf *DEI*, 4, 2602b; *Dict. d'arch. chrét.*, 1624; this competition is on a regional basis: *notarius* in Faenza, *curialis* in Naples (cf *DEI*, 4, 2602b), *tabellio* and *forensis* in Rome and Ravenna (cf Wenger, 745-746), also *exceptor* in Ravenna (cf *DEI*).

Our texts demonstrate a far greater restriction in meaning, in that *notarius* is employed as a secretary in a private sense; this secretary is however in the employ of an ecclesiastical or administrative authority. The division is once again regional: according to Tjäder, 419, *notarius* refers to secretaries of the Church of Ravenna in docs. 4-5 (474-522), and 21 (625), while in 10-11 (Syracuse, 489), it applies to the secretary of King Odoacer. We note in passing that the item also appears in doc. 22 (Ravenna, 639). Although there is some question as to its exact sense, cf Cabrol, *Dict. d'arch. chrét.*, 1633, we note that it appears in a context comparable to that found in doc. 21, where it is found linked with *scriniarius* (whose sense is given variously as 'chancellery official' by Tjäder, 'accountant' in Souter, etc.). Presumably its exclusion from Tjäder's discussion is an oversight.

The periods in which *notarius* is attested in its original and later senses overlap: 'short-hand writer' appears in Gaudentius (4th c.), while 'secretary' or 'scribe' is found in Tertullian (beginning of the 3rd c.), St. Jerome (347-420), and St. Augustine (402), cf Blaise, 558a. In the early citations, no further qualification as to ecclesiastical or royal function is made. Specifically as a church scribe, the attestations are more nearly contemporaneous with doc. 4-5, i. e., the 6th c. (cf Souter, 267a): *notarius* appears as 'clerk in the papal chancery' in Gregory the Great (540-604), the Council of Rome (649), cf Niermeyer, 721b; and in Gregory of Tours (538-594), cf Bonnet, 89.

With reference to 'royal scribe', doc. 10-11 is the earliest attestation of the use. It is however noted shortly thereafter in Gregory the Great (cf Blaise, 558a) and in the Frankish king Childebertus (584), cf Niermeyer, 722a. Apart from this, the remaining Frankish citations noted in Niermeyer are all from a considerably later period, the 9th century. As for the Lombards, however, we find an uninterrupted series of attestations throughout the 7th and 8th centuries as: Ionas (Bobbio, 7th c.), *Codex diplomaticus* of the Longobards (673 and 714), Bertharius (697), Aribertus (706/707), and Paulus Diaconus (ca. 720-ca. 799), cf Niermeyer, 722a. This northern aspect of our attestations continues in the ensuing centuries: Liutprandus (bishop of Cremona; 10th c.), cf Niermeyer; texts from Genoa (Liguria) (946-1230), and Asti (Piedmont, 955-1078), cf Arnaldi. Later references from the 14th c. apply to France, cf Du Cange, 5, 612a (as well as to Finland, cf Hakamies, 114a).

The significance of these attestations for N. Italy and France is all the greater in light of the following forms found in older stages of Romance: old Lomb. *noer* (cf *REW*, 5964, *DEI*, 4, 2602b), old Ven. *nodar (DEI)*, old Prov. *notazy* (cf *FEW*, 7, 199a), old Fr. *notaire* or *notarie* (cf *FEW*, and Godefroy, 5, 533a, and 10, 210b), as well as old Sp. *notario* (cf Corom., 3, 524b). Generally such forms are glossed merely as 'secretary', or 'notary'; it is however Godefroy, 10, 210b, who describes the 13-15th century use (in the C. French department of Loiret, and also in a work on the "Cabochiens" by Coville) as applied to a person in charge of drawing up official acts and who was in the employ of a lord. This is precisely the special sense found in our collection. Finally we point out these dialectal forms which are concentrated in N. Italy: Friul. *nodar* (cf REW, 5964), Venetian *nodaro* (cf Olivieri, 177a), Romagnolan *noder* (cf REW; DEI, 4, 2602b). In addition, the form *noteo* is found in Arezzo, Tuscany (cf REW, DEI), while *notaio* has entered standard It. We conclude that given such a proliferation of dialectal forms, the item penetrated into standard Italian from N. Italy. As for the special sense of 'royal scribe', first employed in our text 10-11, it appears to have been thereafter preserved and transmitted by the Lombards and the Franks, respectively in N. Italy and France. We point out that the fact that 10-11 was written in Sicily is without significance inasmuch as the subject matter concerns Odoacer. Furthermore our other occurrences of *notarius* ('church scribe') are all found in Ravenna texts. It would appear likely that the term originally arose under the impetus of the cultural and religious center of Ravenna, where the need for official and private secretaries was felt. We note, for example, such terms as the following which are derivatives of *notarius*, one of which specifically represented an institution of the Byzantine church: *notariatus* and especially *protonotarius* (the 'first notary'), cf FEW, 7, 200a.

The term is widespread in modern W. Romance in the sense of 'notary public'; it would appear that in Spanish *notarius* was not employed as a 'royal secretary'.

c. *potestas*

Potestas, which has the fundamental sense of 'power, strength', also may be applied in CL in a specialized way to the power or authority of an office. It appears in both senses in our collection, first with reference to legal power in docs. 13 (Ravenna, 553), and 20 (Ravenna, ca. 600), and secondly as a designation of the office of the praetorian prefect in doc. 16 (Ravenna, ca. 600?). It will be observed that our usages span roughly one-half a century. Within about the same period yet a third sense appears, in which *potestas* refers directly the praetorian prefect, in docs. 4-5 (Ravenna, 474-552), and 2 (Ravenna, 565-570). This personal use of the term is analogous to that found in *testimonium*, see page 44. Although the praetorian prefect first was the commander of the imperial body-guard, he served as a provincial governor in the later

Empire (after ca. 366). It is this latter sense which evolves throughout Western Romance and which ultimately takes hold in Italy for designating the chief magistrate, i. e., the mayor, of a city.

Attestations of personal use of *potestas* far antedate our collection: such use appears in Cicero, cf Facciolati-Forcellini, 784a, and in Juvenal, cf Facciolati-Forcellini, and Du Cange, 6, 439c, and subsequently in St. Augustine (386-429), Salvianus (priest of Marseilles, 439-451), cf Blaise, 639a; Du Cange, 6, 437c; the *Codex Theodosianus* (438), and the *Vita* of St. Augustine, written by Possidius (bishop of Calame, Numidia, N. Africa; 430), cf Du Cange. There then ensues a long hiatus until approximately the first half of the 12th century when *potestas* designates an office-holder: Rahewin (canon of Frising, and biographer of Frederick I; 1156-1160), cf Du Cange, 6, 439a; Niermeyer, 820b; in a pact between Frederick and Piacenza (1162), and in a reference to the *principes et potestates* of the Lombards (1183), cf Niermeyer. The use is closely paralleled in the rest of W. Romance at about the same time or thereafter: old Fr. *poestat* 'powerful person, great lord' (cf *REW*, 6697; *FEW*, 9, 255a; *DEI*, 4, 2984b; Godefroy, 6, 241c, who cites a 13th c. Anglo-Norman version of the *Evangile de Nicodème*, as well as the Belgian historian Mouskès of 1215-1283, and a history of Tournai of the 13th-14th c.; also Godefroy, 10, 363a, specifically the sense 'old name of the first magistrate in certain towns of S. France and Italy', however all in late sources of the 16th c.), old Prov. *podestat*, etc. 'governor of a city' (cf *REW; FEW*, 9, 254b; Godefroy; Mistral, 2, 608a, 'elective magistrate'), old Sp. and old Port. forms 'nobles entrusted with the administration of a region' (cf *REW; FEW*, 9, 255a; and Morais, 8, 421a). However it is apparently only in Italy that the form survives specifically as 'mayor' or 'highest magistrate', cf *REW*, 6697; *FEW*, 9, 255a; *DEI*, 4, 2984a. The date at which the item became established in this sense has been placed variously in the late 12th or early 13th centuries. Franchini, *ASI*, 5th ser., 50, 124, observes that it has been thought that the use of the word as applied to the first magistrate of a city arose after Frederick I convened the diet of Roncaglia (1158); he further points out however that others have cited such early instances of use in Bologna and Romagna (1135 and 1151). Note further such use in the following list of C. and N. Italian cities: Arezzo and Pistoia (both in Tuscany, 1153 and 1158), and Bologna (1151-1154), Ferrara (1151), Imola (1153), Reggio (1154), and Faenza (1155) (all of which are in Emilia), cf *Enc. it.*, 27, 578b. Doubtless the establishment of the *podestà* proceeded at an uneven rate in Italy. It came about in particular when the cities of C. and N. Italy underwent, generally in the 12th and 13th centuries, a change from a plural magistracy (including consuls) to one person. By the 13th c. the *podestà* was quite firmly established; however the following late cases indicate that the dual authority still lingered: in a peace treaty between the Pisans and the emir of Tunis (1264) reference is made to the *podestade* as well as to the consuls, cf Monaci, 167; Sella also cites *potestas seu consules* (Viterbo, C. It., 1251), *GLI*, 358.

Generally however the usage is firmly entrenched from the 13th and 14th centuries on: we note the frequent use in Lombardy, cf Bosshard, 90, 141, 159, 165, 244, 325. Dialectally the use is also attested in old Lomb. *poestae*, cf Salvioni, *AGl*, 12, 422; *FEW*, 9, 255a. The preponderance of northern citations is by now evident. We conclude by observing that our texts show, in addition to the classical sense, a step in the evolution from military governor to mayor. A possible direct connection may be inferred between our texts and the first attestations in the 12th century, since they both originate in the same area. On the other hand, our texts are no more pertinent with regard to the specific sense of mayor than they are to the parallel early evolution in sense in old Fr., Prov., Sp. and Port. What argues against a direct connection between our documents and the later use in Italy is the fact that a very long period of time transpires during which we have no documentation of change.

4.2. SUMMARY

Of the three forms, *mansionarius, notarius,* and *potestas,* only the first is a non-CL form, though it is derived by the same process which produced *notarius*. The main importance of the words lies in their evolution in sense necessitated by the changing requirements of the social organization. Only *notarius* appears for the first time in our collection in the specific sense studied here. As for citations in medieval Latin, both *mansionarius* and *notarius* are well attested, the former in particular with regard to Rome, and Germany, the latter with regard to the Lombards and the Franks. Between our citations of *potestas* there elapses a long time before those of the mid-12th c. A geographical connection is likewise noted in the case of *mansionarius* and *notarius* between the regions in which they appear in our texts (respectively Rome and Ravenna). In the case of *potestas,* however, such an apparent relationship between Ravenna and the later citations from Emilia is suspect in that there is no intervening supporting evidence, and in addition, the sense of our texts is just as pertinent with reference to other early Romance forms, where geography is not a question. Furthermore, with regard to the dialectal attestations, only in the case of *notarius* and its reflexes in old Lomb. and the modern N. dialects, may we speak of a very likely correlation with our texts. The connections between N. Italy or Rhaetia and *mansionarius* and *potestas* appear largely coincidental. Finally with regard to Western Romance, we have noted in each of the items parallel early semantic developments (old Fr. *maisnier* "servant'; old Fr. and old Prov. *notaire,* etc. 'scribe attached to a lord'; and the frequent reflexes of *potestas* 'governor', etc.). It is finally to be observed however that these senses are preserved in the case of *mansionarius* and *potestas* only in Italy and Rhaetia.

5.1. Widespread in Italy, and in Romance

a. *soca*

Various suppositions have been made as to the origin of It. *soga.* Basque and especially Keltic have been suggested, cf Diez, 297; Thurneysen, 79; Körting, *Lat.-Rom. Wörterb.,* 896; Prati, in *It. dial.,* 13, 167. Ascoli related *soga* to Sanskrit *sagg* (cited in Prati, *It. dial.*). (For other suppositions, cf Olivieri, 648a, who derives *soca* from a non-CL *sauca* 'little rope', presumably from a root * *seu-* or * *su-* based on CL *suere* 'to sew', and Monlau y Roca, 1050a, who cites Covarrubias' belief that the original form was Hebraic!) Despite an earlier predilection for Keltic, however, modern scholarship is somewhat more uncertain and notes only the possibility of such an origin, cf *REW*, 8051; *DEI*, 5, 3528a; Corom., 4, 266b. Nonetheless the form is found widespread in Western Romance: old Fr. *soue, seuwe*, etc. (cf *REW; DEI;* Bertoni, 9; Godefroy, 7, 409b), Walloon *sawe, sowe* (in the region of Neufchâteau and the Haute Semois, in Luxembourg (cf Haust, 228, *REW*); old Prov., Cat., Sp., and Port. *soga* (cf *REW; DEI;* Bertoni; Morais, 10, 319a; Monlau y Roca, 1050a). The item is particularly well attested in Italy, in modern dialects as well as in late and medieval Latin. Although it may be presumed that the modern forms could have spread from an innovating center, thus to occur in regions which likely do not have a Keltic substratum, our collection is particularly notable for the fact that it offers the first citation of the form, in doc. 8 (564) which originates in an area (Ravenna) normally not associated with the Keltic substratum. The form is subsequently quite well attested, as: *Edictus* of Rotharus (Lombardic king; 643; *si quis sogas furaverit de bovis iunctorios*), cf Diez, 297; Du Cange, 7, 508b; Arnaldi; a document from Rome (756), cf *DEI*, 5, 3528a; Sella, *GLI*, 536; the *Codex Cavensis* (Salerno, in Campania; 9th c.), cf de Bartholomaeis, in *AGl*, 15, 362; the *Liber Legis Longobardorum Papiensis* (Pavia, 9th c.; *si sogas furatus fuerit de bove*), cf Arnaldi; *DEI*, 5, 3528a; Corom., 4, 266a. Other citations are from a considerably later period: Bologna (Emilia, 1159), cf *DEI;* Sella, *GLE*, 329; Imola (Emilia, 1197), cf *DEI, GLE;* Pope Innocent III (died 1216), cf Diez, 297; Du Cange, 7, 508b; Treviso (Venetia; 1313, 1315, 1334), cf Sella, *GLI*, 536. The earliest attestation in Italian (Dante, 1265-1321) hence appears at about the same time as the later Latin citations, cf Prati, in *It. dial.*, 13, 167.

It is apparent from the citations that occurrences in the north predominate, the sole exceptions being 8th and 9th c. instances from Rome and Salerno. Indeed, our sources are in general agreement as to the northern provenance of the word, cf *REW*, 8051; *DEI*, 5, 3528a; Bertoni, 9. The modern dialectal distribution is highly corroborative of this, although there is not an inconsiderable attestation for the south as well. AIS 242 'rope' shows the following: (Rheto-Romance) Western (sixteen points), Central (P. 311, 323), Friul. (P. 326); (North) Lomb. (P. 286), Ven. (eight points), Emilia (P. 444, 453); (South) Apulia (nine points), Basilic.

(P. 732, 733, 735, 744), Camp. (P. 725, 731), Calab. (P. 745). The situation in Calabria is also confirmed by Rohlfs, *Diz. dial.*, 2, 421, while Olivieri, 648a, confirms the attestations for N. Italy, Friul., and Apulia. The remaining maps of the *AIS* present the following: 250 'rope on a pulley': (North) Emilia (P. 444); 267 'girth': (North) Alpine Lomb. (P. 53), Pied. (P. 109), (South) Apulia (P. 716); 546 'fagot band': (South) Molise (P. 656), Apulia (P. 728); (Sardinia) (P. 937, 938); 1191 'yoke, collar': (Central) Tusc. (P. 571); 1234 'saddle-girth': (North) Lomb. (P. 244); 1236 'cow rope': (South) Camp. (P. 731), Basilic. (P. 735); 1243 'whip, lash': (Central) Tusc. (P. 581); 1470 'part of a flail': (North) Lig. (P. 189), Lomb. (P. 225); 1565 'tie (string, band)': (South) Apulia (P. 719). The foregoing is summarized thus in terms of total attestations: Rheto-Romance (19), North (17), Central (2), South (22), Sardinian (2).

A striking division between North and South is immediately discerned. The Rheto-Roman and certain of the northern forms appear to confirm a previous Keltic influence. Furthermore the two points in Emilia are particularly impressive in that they both occur near Ravenna and Bologna where we have noted earlier citations. However the attestations in S. Italy are surprisingly strong in number, while central Italy is almost completely ignored. (We note in passing also that the specialized sense 'cow-rope' which was found in the Longobardic citations noted above appears dialectally only in the south.) We suggest the following explanation of this undeniably heavy attestation in the south: *soca*, very likely of Keltic origin, entered Latin in N. Italy, and thence spread with the language of the new capital Ravenna throughout C. and S. Italy. Citations in medieval Latin from Rome and especially Salerno attest to this; since S. Italy is extremely conservative, the form is still attested there today.

With regard to phonology it is noted that doc. 8 shows *soca*, which is undoubtedly a hypercorrective form in light of the g (or y or effacement) which is characteristic of all of the northern forms (with the exception of *AIS* 1470, P. 225), as well as in the rest of W. Romance. Similarly k prevails in C. and S. Italy (with one exception in *AIS* 242, P. 732), and Sardinia. (For a discussion of k or kk in the Nuorese form, cf Wagner, 2, 423b.) Given the clear-cut distribution in Italy, it hardly seems arguable that *soca* represents the older form. Further cf Flechia, in *AGl*, 3, 143, who favors this view. The retention of the voiceless intervocalic stop in S. Italy and Sardinia supports this. The actual occurrence in Ravenna is a remembrance of an earlier form.

b. *spatharius*

For the derivation of non-CL *spatharius* 'swordbearer' from CL *spatha* 'sword', compare our remarks for *mansionarius*, page 33. The item appears in doc. 16 (Ravenna, ca. 600?), and hence is antedated by a sizable number of other attestations, as: in various inscriptions from the 4th-5th c. on, cf Souter, 383a; Idatius (bishop of Chaves, in Galicia; 395-470), cf Blaise, 768a; the *Collectio Avellana* (a collection of material concerning Roman and Byzantine magistrates, etc.; 367-553), cf Blaise, and Souter; the Burgundian Laws (end of the 5th c.), cf Du Cange, 7, 545a; Cassiodorus (Calabria; ca. 480-ca. 575), cf Blaise, Souter; Gregory the Great (593), cf Blaise, Souter. Later occurrences are as follows: Pope Leo III (795-816), cf Arnaldi; gloss from 690-750 or the 10th c., cf *CGL*, 5, 166, 9; Anastasius (9th c.), cf Du Cange, 7, 545a; gloss from the 16th c. attributed to Isidore and based on 9th c. material, cf *CGL*, 5, 589, 15 (very possibly the same as that attributed to Papias, grammarian possibly from Pavia, who died in 1053, cf Du Cange); gloss from the 10th c., cf *CGL*, 3, 509, 73; text from Amalfi (Campania, 922), cf Arnaldi; text from Conversano (Apulia, indeterminate date), cf Arnaldi; Aelfric (England, died in 1006), cf Du Cange; Lucas Tudensis (bishop of Tuy, in Galicia; died ca. 1250), cf Du Cange; text from Bologna (1283), cf Sella, *GLE*, 331; *spadarius*. (A citation possibly to be attributed to one Pelagius, son of Duke Fafila, otherwise unidentifiable as to place or time, is also noted by Du Cange.) The item is attested in early Romance in old Pisan *spataro*, cf *DEI*, 5, 3580b, and in old It. (Dante) *spadaio*, cf *DEI*, 5, 3573b. It is the latter form, along with *spadaro*, which is found in standard Italian. Both the intervocalic stops and the endings of these forms merit treatment. While the voiceless stop of the Pisan form is to be expected, the -*d*- of the remaining forms suggests a N. origin. However, the old It. form in -*aio* represents the typical development of CL

-*arius*, cf Rohlfs, *Hist. Gramm.*, 1, 465, and 3, 282, 320; hence the form appears to be a mixture of northern and standard features. In similar manner, the forms in -*aro* are more typically associated with the north, Rohlfs, 3, 282. The form *spadaro* hence is apparently a direct descendant of a northern form, very possibly to be associated with *spatharius* in our text. As for the rest of the Romania, *espadero* is cited only in Sp., cf Monlau y Roca, 676a, and Corom., 2, 380b, who names as his source the following work: Alonso Fernández de Palencia, *Universal vocabulario en latín y en romance*, Seville, 1490. We further cite a treatment of the work in Hill, who notes, 70, the following: *Amger en vulgar es espadero* (which is incidentally practically identical with certain citations of the *CGL*, for references see above).

We conclude that on the basis of the intervocalic stops and the endings seen in certain It. forms there may be a connection with our text. We further point out however that citations of *spatharius* occur well before our collection and in widely diverse areas of Italy. We note with interest however the possible link between the two citations in Galicia (Idatius, Lucas of Tuy), a very conservative region of the Iberian peninsula, and the subsequent Sp. form.

c. *testimonium*

We have previously treated the personalized use of *potestas*, see page 37; *testimonium* undergoes a like semantic evolution from 'testimony' to 'witness'. Syntactically the use is explained by Meyer-Lübke, *Gramm.*, 3, 159, as arising from an abl. followed by a gen. (presumably 'in whose witnesship'), while Gamillscheg, *Etym.*, 838a, suggests a conflation of *testimonio esse* and *testem esse*. Spitzer, in *Arch. Rom.*, 22, 372ff, rejects both of these arguments, based as they are on a presumed misunderstanding on the part of speakers of the language, and declares that the use arises merely from metonymy, i. e., the application of a function to the person exercising that function. Also cf Löfstedt, *LL*, 152, nt. 1.

Interestingly, while both *testimonium* and *testis* occur in our collection, it is *testimonium* which is chronologically first, in doc. 1 (Ravenna, 445-446). Thereafter, *testis* is overwhelmingly the prevalent form, as in the following texts which are all from Ravenna unless otherwise indicated: 4-5 (474-552), 13 (553), 8 (564), 14-15 (572), 6 (575), 16 (ca. 600?), 20 (ca. 600), 17 (Rome, ca. 600?), 18-19 (Rome, ca. 600?), 28 (613-641), 21 (625), 22 (639), 25 (lst half of the 7th c.?), 24 (mid-7th c.), and 23 (ca. 700?). Thus it would appear that *testimonium* is a chance early occurrence; *testis* seemingly preserves its strength in our collection. However, it is noted that the latter appears largely in legal formularies, whose conservatism may account for some of its perseverance.

Testimonium 'witness' is first attested in the *Peregrinatio* (Spain, 383), cf Fraenkel, in *Glotta*, 4, 47; Stolz-Schmalz, 367; Löfstedt, *Phil. Komm.*, 332; Blaise, 814b. Other early citations which precede or fall right after our doc. 1 are: Sulpicius Severus (Bordeaux, ca. 360-413), Evagrius (ca. 430), Paulinus Petricordiensis (Périgueux, born 470); and the *Lex Salica* (6th c.), cf Löfstedt. *Verm.*, 212f. Co-occurrence of *testis* and *testimonium* also characterizes the *Lex Salica* (cf Eckhardt, 100, who cites such phrases as *de falso testimonium*), as well as Liutprandus (Cremona, 726), cf Löfstedt, *Verm.*, 212; Heraeus, in *GGA*, 177, 473. We find a striking parallel in time between these citations and our collection in that both forms may appear between the 4th and the 8th centuries.

Subsequent attestations are frequent, as: a text dated 779, but otherwise not identified as to place, cf Du Cange, 8, 87a; text from Pisa (796), cf Arnaldi; text from Venetia (845), cf Arnaldi; annotation on the *Codex Justinianus* (beginning of the 9th c.), cf Arnaldi; an old *placitum* (otherwise unidentified as to place, 869), cf Du Cange; *Codex Cavensis* (Salerno, 9th c.), cf Arnaldi; a text from Rome (988), cf Arnaldi; a document from Farfa (Latium, 1106-1118), cf Du Cange; a document of Burchardus (bishop of Worms, ca. 965-ca. 1025), cf Du Cange. (In addition, Du Cange cites other sources in Burgundy and Germany, which are unidentified as to date.) Citations which are considerably later are from Ragusa (1363), cf Sella, *GLI*, 222; Rome (1363), cf *GLI*, 368; Finland (1372), cf Hakamies, 177a; and Verona (1450), cf *GLI*, 368.

It is apparent that in both the early and late attestations a relatively large geographical area is involved. As for Italy, the form appears in the south as well as in the north. In the Romania, however, it is striking how many of the citations originate in

Western Romance, especially in France, but also in Spain (the first citation) and N. Italy. Early and modern Romance largely reflect this distribution.

Possibly the earliest Romance use appears in the *Glosas Emilianenses* (Spain, 11th c.), cf Spitzer, in *Arch. Rom.*, 22, 374. Other early Romance uses occur in old Campid. (Sardinia; cf *REW*, 8685; *DEI*, 5, 3776a), and especially in old Fr. *tesmoing* (cf *REW; DEI;* and Godefroy, 10, 759a, who further notes in 7, 699b, that the form also retained the sense 'testimony').

The following situation prevails in modern Italy where both *testimone* and *testimonio* may appear in the standard language as 'witness', cf Körting, *Lat.-Rom. Wörterb.*, 956; *DEI*, 5, 3776a. (*Testimonio*, which is doubtless a Latinism, more often appears as 'testimony", however.) Dialectally, reflexes of *testimonium* are generalized throughout Italy and Sardinia, cf *REW*, 8685; *DEI; DES*, 2, 479b; the Campid., Sass., and Nuor. forms enjoy the double meaning. (As for W. Rheto-Romance, a rival form, *párdecá*, etc., from *perduco, perductus, -um?*, prevails, cf *AIS*, 737.)

Reflexes are widespread in the rest of Western Romance, although a double meaning is frequently possible as: Fr. *témoin*, Prov. 'testimony' or "witness' (cf Mistral, 2, 983b, who notes that the sense 'witness' is old), Sp. *testimonio* (cf Corom., 4, 435b) or *testimonia* (cf Körting, 956; Löfstedt, *Phil. Komm.*, 332), Cat. (cf Alcover-Moll, 271), and Port. *testemunha* (cf *REW*, 8685; Fraenkel, in *Glotta*, 4, 46-47; Morais, 10, 833a). Certain of the forms merit comment. It is likely that the Cat. form is a Latinism, cf Alcover-Moll. Furthermore, according to Corominas, the sense of 'witness' is rare for Sp. *testimonio*. Finally, it is noted that in both Sp. and Port. it is the original neuter plural which may give rise to the Romance form in *-a;* in Port., *testemunho* retains the original sense 'testimony', cf Morais, 10, 835a and 836b.

By way of summation, we note that reflexes of *testimonium* are very frequent throughout Italy and most of Western Romance, both in the standard languages as well as in the dialects of Italy and Sardinia. According to our evidence it would appear that the early attestations originate in Spain, France and N. Italy. It is especially striking that both the earliest late Latin form and that of Romance should be situated in Spain. For a general note on the overall conservatism of the Spanish lexicon; cf Menéndez Pidal, 7. We have further documented the rivalry between *testis* and *testimonium;* although *testis* ultimately loses out to *testimonium,* it cannot be said that *testimonium* necessarily loses its classical sense. In several instances (old Fr., mod. Sard.) we have indicated that it stands for both "testimony" and 'witness'. In other cases (Sp., Port.) a morphological difference based on gender serves to distinguish the meanings; compare Fr. *témoignage,* presumably from a suffixed form **testimoniaticum,* cf Körting, *Lat.-Rom. Wörterb.,* 956.

d. *sarica*

Sarica (variant *sareca*) 'silk dress', while technically non-CL, quite evidently belongs to CL *sericum* 'silk'. It is likely that long *e* underwent a change to *a* under the influence of the subsequent *r* (as possibly occurs elsewhere in the collection, *Marcator,* etc.), cf Tjäder, 434. However a purely lexical explanation is also possible of contamination with *sagum,* cf Corom., 2, 1048b, and Gamillscheg, *Etym.,* 798a. Whichever the cause, we venture that the form *sarica* of doc. 8 was no longer identified by the scribe with *sericum.* Note the changes effected in related words, *olosiricoprata* 'silk merchant' (in different stress position) in doc. 4-5, and especially in *tramosirica* 'half-silk' which occurs also in doc. 8 in close proximity to *sarica.* Hence we shall treat *sarica* in distinction to other possible late forms commencing with *seri-* or *siri-*.

With regard to the variant *sareca,* we note with interest that our sources have considered it as an attested form, whereas they have most usually marked *sarica* with an asterisk, cf Körting, *Lat.-Rom. Wörterb.,* 880; *REW,* 7848; *DEI,* 5, 3342b; Prati, 865a; and Rohlfs, *Hist. Gramm.,* 2, 217. It is our view that this practice began as a lapse on the part of Körting, then to be perpetuated by others, for we note that in an earlier source (Diez, 281), the form was not marked thus.

The two alternant forms, *sarica* and *sareca,* appear for the first time in doc. 8 (Ravenna, 564); the variant *sareca* appears very shortly thereafter in the *Itinerarium* of Antoninus (a description of a trip to holy places, ca. 570), cf Blaise, 739b; Souter, 364b.

Other citations are from considerably later times: a text from Tuscany (792), cf Arnaldi; Niermeyer, 938b; a *Vita* of St. Eligius (mid- 8th c.), cf Niermeyer; *Liber Pontificalis* of Benedictus III (855-858), cf Niermeyer; the *Chronica* of St. Benedictus (9th-10th c.), cf Arnaldi and Niermeyer; and in Leo Ostiensis (Ostia, in Latium; 1046-1115), cf Niermeyer, and Du Cange, 7, 311c. It is apparent that attestations from C. Italy predominate.

As for early Romance, we cite the following: old It. *sarga* (cf *DEI*, 5, 3342b); an 11th c. set of glosses in Rheto-Romance and German: *sarga vel vestido, roc* (cf Monaci, 524); old Fr. *sarga* (cf *REW*, 7848; *DEI*, 5, 3342b; Godefroy, 10, 665c; Corom., 2, 1048b; Olivieri, 638a); old Prov. *sargua* 'serge material' (cf Körting, *Lat.-Rom. Wörterb.*, 880; Gröber, in *Archiv. f. lat. Lexicog. u. Gramm.*, 5, 466; Puşcariu; Em. Levy, 7, 473a) or *sarga* (cf Corom., Levy). (We note that Levy and Raynouard, 5, 155b, cite respectively the parallel forms *serga* and *sarga* in the same author, Guilhem de Durfort.) In modern Romance the item appears, with some differentiation and evolution in sense, in Sp. *sarga* 'kind of woollen material, cloth with weave in diagonal lines' (cf *REW*; *DEI*; Corom., 2, 1048a), and Rum. *sarică* (*REW*; Puşcariu, 'shaggy peasant's coat'). (It is generally agreed that the forms found in It., Cat., and Port. are from Fr., cf *REW*, *DEI*, Olivieri, 638a, Corom., Gröber, Morais, 9, 926b and 929a; however it may be noted incidentally that Alcover-Moll, fasc. 169, 756a, derive the Cat. form via an intermediary Arabic *saraga*.) Finally a collateral masc. form *sargo*, which refers to a kind of cloth, is cited for Prov., cf Mistral, 2, 847a.

As far as the dialectal situation of Italy is concerned we find a considerable shift in locale, as well as great variety in sense, as: (Central) *sarga* (Rieti, cf *REW*, 7848; *DEI*, 5, 3342b), *sarga* 'pocket inside coat or petticoat' (Amiata, in S. Tusc.; cf *DEI*); (South) *sarga* or *saia* (Calab., cf *DEI*, Olivieri, 638a), also *sarica* 'coat of coarse material with big pockets'; and *sarga* "kind of light material' (Calab.; Rohlfs, *Hist. Gramm.*, 2, 217 and 218). It may be noted that the *DEI* assigns the meaning 'coat of coarse material, etc.' to a parallel derivative *sáraca* in Calab. (Lastly we note in passing the form *salico* 'jacket of rough material", from Cervara, near Rome, cited in *REW*; it is apparently a direct derivative of *sericum*, or possibly represents a masc. re-formation of *sarica*.)

In summation, we have noted that the item appears in a large area of the Romania, in the east (Rumania), as well as the west (especially Iberia; in N. France the form appears to have lost out to rival forms deriving from *seri-*). As for Italy, there is very little geographical correlation between Ravenna and the other citations whether Latin or dialectal. Further we register our grave doubts with regard to Tjäder's translation of *sarica* as 'silk clothing'. We have shown that the item was kept formally distinct from other items which pertained more immediately to silk. Furthermore, the evolution of the term in the Romania indicates something much coarser, cf Niermeyer, 938b. Finally, the item is glossed in other sources merely as 'kind of tunic", cf Du Cange, 7, 311c; Sella, *GLE*, 306; Blaise, 739b; Arnaldi.

5.2. SUMMARY

Of the four forms treated here, *soca, spatharius, testimonium,* and *sarica*, we have seen that all except *spatharius* are widespread in the Romania. *Sarica* enjoys the greatest geographical spread, appearing in both eastern and western Romance, while *soca* and *testimonium* appear in Italy and W. Romance. *Spatharius*, on the other hand, survives only in standard Italian and Spanish. As for the dialects of Italy, Rhaetia and Sardinia, *soca* appears very frequently and indeed makes a surprisingly strong showing in S. Italy. *Testimonium* is the generalized form for "witness' except in W. Rheto-Romance. Finally *sarica* occurs sporadically in C. and S. Italy, but is surprisingly lacking in the north.

Three forms, *soca, spatharius* and *sarica*, are non-CL in origin; however the last two are easily derived from classical forms. On the basis of its distribution in Italy and W. Romance, we are inclined to attribute *soca* to a substratum influence. However despite its seeming pertinence the preservation of intervocalic -k- is of little help inasmuch as it is normally retained in S. It. and Sard. The same is also true for Basque, cf Rohlfs, "*Bask. Kult.*", 85. Hence it is not possible to ascertain whether the Basque form is itself the original form or whether Basque adopted the word from the local early Roman speech. The latter view seems more likely.

Two forms, *soca* and *sarica*, appear for the first time in Latin in doc. 8. *Testimonium* in the sense of 'witness' and *spatharius* occur as early as the 4th century.

Finally we have noted discrepancies in past scholarship both in regard to the employment of an asterisk with *sarica* and to the interpretation of its meaning.

D. Groups of semantically related items with characteristic distribution in Italy

The following study concerns pairs or groups of items which bear a partial semantic identity and which we have examined in terms of their semantic evolution and present geographical distribution especially in Italy. The groups contain both classical and non-CL forms. Finally we note the fact that upon occasion we find that all of the members of a particular group are found in a single document. Despite the fact that this by definition may nullify the concept of dialectal division within our collection, we nonetheless have examined such forms in light of their subsequent distribution.

1.1. Vessels and containers

We note in doc. 8 (Ravenna, 564), between the lines 2-5 and 2-13, the following concentration of vessels of various types, cited here with their usual CL or LL acceptation: (CL) *alveolus* 'tray, trough, basin', *alveus* 'deep vessel, basket, tray', *catinus* 'dish, bowl', *concha* 'vessel for wine', *cucumella* 'little cook-pot', *panarium* 'bread-basket', *olla* 'pot', *orca* 'butt, tun', *scutella* 'salver', *urceolus* 'pitcher'; (non-CL) *buttis* 'barrel', *butticella* "little barrel', *caccabellus* 'small cook-pot', *cuppus* (CL *cupa* 'tun, cask'), and *tina* 'wine-vessel'. We point out however that examination of the contexts necessarily reveals differentiations in sense: *butte granaria* (*butte de cito* also occurs), *tina clusa*, and *butticella granaria.* (Other of the contexts merely corroborate or do not materially change the usual senses: *orca olearia, conca aerea, orciolus aereus* and *testeus, albiolus ligneus,* and *olla testea.*)

A major division may be drawn separating the larger objects from the smaller: *buttis, orca, tina, conca, butticella* vs. *scutella, cucumella, orciolus, catinus, albiolus, caccavellus,* and *panarium.* (We withhold classification of *cuppus.*) Similarly it is observed that the first group generally refers to items normally associated with liquid measure; obvious deviations are apparent however in the case of *buttis* (liquid and dry measure), and *butticella* (dry measure only). Furthermore, *tina* which is normally considered a tun or a vat, i. e., open at the top, is specified as *clusa,* and hence is akin to a barrel.

1.2. SMALL

Of the small vessels cited, two merit special attention.

a. *caccabellus*

From the standpoint of derivation, *caccabellus* is quite obviously a non-CL diminutive of CL *cac(c)abus* 'cooking pot'. Hence it appears in place of CL *cac(c)abulus.* The item appears for the first time in doc. 8 (Ravenna, 564) in the guise *caccavello.* The base form has been treated as a hypothetical form in *REW,* 1444; and Gröber, in *Archiv f. lat. Lexicog. und Gramm.,* 1, 539. This is justifiable in terms of our document which has *-v-* for *-b-;* however forms with *-b-* do occur later, as we note below.

A virtually contemporary citation occurs in Oribasius (6th c.), cf Souter, 34; Arnaldi; and Svennung, 68. It also appears much later in the *Codex Cavensis* (Salerno, written between 792-1069, cf de Bartholomaeis, in *AGl,* 15, 334, *caccabelli*).

In the Romania, the most notable continuator of the item outside of Italy appears in old Fr. *cachevel* (or *ch-*) 'skull', and *caquevel* 'summit, peak', cf *REW,* 1444; *FEW,* 2, 21a; *DEI,* 1, 642a; Godefroy, 2, 30a; *ThesLL,* 3, 5, 4ff; and especially Schuchardt, in *Zeit. f. rom. Phil.,* 24, 568. (Note the semantic parallel with *testa,* cf Cornu, in *Romania,* 11, 109. Also compare German *Kopf,* cf Kluge, 392b and Löfstedt, *LL,* 26f).

As for Italy, very few instances may be found of reflexes which are appropriate in both form and meaning. A parallel fem. *cacabella 'casseruola'* (Teramo, N. Abruzzi; 1365) is cited in Sella, *GLI,* 649, and *DEI,* 1, 642a. As for modern Italy, but oné instance is noted in *AIS* 955, *kwakkwavídd* 'earthen kettle', in Apulia (P. 718). Our collection indicates that the form was geographically more widespread in the late 6th c.

b. *cucumella*

The history of *cucumella, REW,* 2361, is closely parallel to that of *caccabellus.* It is a diminutive of CL *cucuma* 'kettle', and appears in doc. 8 (Ravenna, 564). The principal differentiation between the two objects is the fact that the *caccavello* weighs one pound, the *cucumella* one and one-half. *Cucumella* is little attested; it appears once in Alfenus (consul, BC 38), cf *ThesLL,* 4, 1282, 9. In the Romania, it is restricted solely to Italy where it appears dialectally in widely separated regions, Pied. *cucumela* (cf *FEW,* 2, 1457a) and *kukumę̱lla* 'earth pot' or 'pitcher or jar', in Sonnino (S. Latium), cf *AIS* 955 and 967 (P. 682). As was the case above, doc. 8 is indicative of the fact that the item, which is now greatly limited in occurrence, at one time was more widely distributed in Italy.

1.3. LARGE

c. *buttis*

Buttis is a LL neologism which is employed today throughout the Romania in the sense of 'barrel'. Its association with wine or vinegar is clearly seen in citations in *ThesLL,* 2, 2260, 65ff; de Bartholomaeis, *AGl,* 15, 333; *CGL,* 4, 218, 11; Arnaldi; Rački, 18; Niermeyer, 111a. In doc. 8, *buttis* has a dual function in that it serves as a container for vinegar as well as for grain. Although we find (in a related form *botas*) a reference in Niermeyer to honey, we find none in the literature in which grain is specified.

Presumably two containers were meant, one akin to a barrel, the other something like a basket or hamper.

d. *butticella*

Butticella, obviously a non-CL diminutive formation of the preceding, rivals the more usual *butticula* (Fr. *bouteille*, It. *bottiglia*). (Compare other similar occurrences in *horticellus, sagellum,* and *domucella*, pages 21, 30, 67.) It is notable for the fact that it is adopted by standard Italian in the form *botticella* 'small cask or barrel', cf *DEI*, 1, 576b; *FEW*, 1, 660a. However, in our collection it parallels *buttis* in that it is employed as a dry measure.

The item is first attested in doc. 8 (Ravenna, 564). Citations from later times are relatively frequent and are found mainly in Emilia: in a *charta* from Bologna (1227), cf Sella, *GLE,* 56; in the *memoriali* of *notai* from Bologna (13th c.), cf Monaci, 290; and texts from Ravenna (15th and 16th c.), cf Sella, *GLE*. Dialectally the form is rivalled by a parallel masc. formation with which it is easily confused (for example, *botezöl* in Bergamo, cited in *REW*, 1427). The fem. form is preserved in Venetia at two points (P. 327, 374), cf *AIS* 1325. The connection with N. Italy is a certainty; indeed, we have shown that the form is transmitted primarily in documents from Ravenna or nearby.

e. *tina*

Like *buttis, tina* is a pan-Romance form. As for its history its appearance in doc. 8 (Ravenna, 564) is possibly antedated by one early occurrence: Nonius Marcellus (born AD 280) cites the use in Varro (died BC 27), cf Du Cange, 8, 108a. The item appears frequently from the 6th c. on: Oribasius (6th c.), cf Souter, 415a; the *Codex Cavensis* (Salerno; between 792-1069), cf de Bartholomaeis, in *AGl,* 15, 360; the glosses of Cassel (OHG and Romance, 8th c.), cf Monaci, 552. References abound in Du Cange, 8, 108a with regard to a variety of places especially in N. Italy and S. France (Vercelli, in the Piedmont; Dauphiné, Marseilles, etc.); however most are unidentified as to date. Indeed, Monaci, 552, notes that the item was long considered French in origin, but is now thought to be Friulan. Northern provenance is supported by attestations from Venetia (13th c.), cf Monaci, 388, and from Lombardy (1392), cf Bosshard, 128.

Of the items treated here *tina*, apart from *buttis*, is by far the best attested dialectal form in Italy and Rhaetia. The following is a resume of its distribution in its most pertinent senses as seen in the *AIS:* 1319 'vat, measure': (North) Ven. (P. 352, 368); (Central) Umbria (P. 576); (South) Apul. (P. 728, 737); 1321 'large vat used in fermenting': (Rheto-Romance) Grisons (P. 58), (North) Lomb. or W. Rheto-Romance (P. 45, 46), Alpine Lomb. (P. 41, 52, 53, 71, 73, 93), Pied. (30 points), Lomb. (22 points), Lig. (P. 184, 185, 187, 189, 193, 199), Ven. (eight points), Emilia (eight points); (Central) Tusc. (P. 500, 553, 554, 572, 581, 582), Marche (P. 536, 578), Umbria (P. 546, 555, 564, 574, 583, 584), Latium (P. 603, 612, 630, 632, 633); (South) Abr. (P. 608), Camp. (P. 712, 713, 725, 731), Apulia (P. 718, 727), Basilic. (P. 733, 744), Calab. (P. 745, 751, 752, 771); 1321 'two-handled tub': (South) Abr.-Mol. (P. 618, 619, 639), Apulia (P. 708, 709, 718), Camp. (P. 714, 740). Other maps with a connection with wine or grapes are: 1318 'vessel in which grapes are pressed': (Central) Umbria (P. 583), Tusc. (P. 572); 1320 'wine press': (North) Ven. (P. 381), (South) Apulia (P. 707), Calab. (P. 760); 1351 'a pressing tub or vat': (South) Abr.-Mol. (P. 658); 1352 'earthen vessel placed in pit before wine press': (South) Abr.-Mol. (P. 608); 1486 'tub or vat in shape of fermentation vat': (South) Camp. (P. 713).

It is apparent that the item is attested dialectally throughout Italy. In its most typical sense, wine vat used in fermentation, it is heavily concentrated in the wine growing areas of the north.

f. *cuppus*

We have reserved treatment of *cuppus* until this point as there is some question as to its sense. It is quite evidently a masc. derivative of CL *cupa* 'tub, cask, tun, vat' (*REW*, 2401; de Cihac, 69), a form which early is rivalled by *cuppa* (*REW*, 2409; de Cihac, 653). Though obviously related, the two etyma account variously for Romance reflexes which may be grouped very broadly into tubs and goblets or cups (Fr. *cuve* and *coupe*). Despite the geminate *p* in *cuppus* 'tun, cask', it shows greater semantic affinity with *cupa;* originally there was no doubt an instance of a change in declension from a 1st feminine to a 2nd masculine form, a change which is accounted for thus: since certain nouns in *-a* are associated with the notions of collectivity or large size, formations in *-o* refer to something smaller. Cf Meyer-Lübke, *Gramm.*, 2, 476; Rohlfs, *Hist. Gramm.*, 2, 85. Since we bar the notion of 'glass, cup' on the grounds of contextual implausibility, *cuppo (cupo)* must hence have the sense of a small vat or tub. It thus rivals *buttis* (especially *buttis minor*); however as we have seen it doubtless is distinct from *butticella* used as a dry measure. It is probably smaller than the usual *tina,* and in terms of doc. 8 where the *tina* is *clusa* it is obviously a different type of vessel.

Early attestations of the masc. form *cup(p)us* are indeed infrequent. Doc. 8 (Ravenna, 564), represents the first or almost the first, along possibly with an occurrence in Isidore, XX, vi, 7 (Spain; ca. 560-ca. 640), cf *CGL*, 5, 566, 29; *ThesLL*, 4, 1410, 46; Corom., 1, 959a. (Du Cange, 2, 660c, likewise notes *cupus* in a text from Vercelli, in the Piedmont; however the date is indeterminate and in addition the sense refers to a grain measure.)

Citations are likewise rare in early Romance. The following are noted in old It.: 'measure of volume', from Bagnoregio (in Latium; 1373), and from Atri (province of Teramo, in the Abruzzi; 16th c.), cf Sella, *GLI,* 551 and 655; *DEI,* 2, 1097b. (The form is likewise attested in the sense of a grain measure in Fermo, in the Marche, in the 16th c., cf Sella, *GLI,* 175.) Elsewhere these early Romance forms are noted: old Prov. *cup* '*cuve*', cf *FEW,* 2, 1550a; old Sp. *cubo* '*cuba*', cf Corom., 1, 959a; and old Cat. *cup* or *cop,* in a variety of senses, 'kind of bowl', 'dry measure', 'wine vat', etc., cf Corom., Alcover-Moll, 3, 495a, and 854a. Similar reflexes are attested today in France (Vosges, Montauban, Aveyron, etc.), Switzerland (Bern, Neuchâtel), cf *FEW,* 2, 1548b; Prov. *cub* '*cuve*', and *cubo* '*vessel for crushing grapes*', cf Mistral, 1, 684b and 685b; Cat., cf Alcover-Moll, 3, 854a; and Port. *copo* '*glass, goblet*', and *cubo* 'large hamper used for grapes' (in Alentejo), etc., cf Morais, 3, 526b and 734b. (It will be noted that the large variety of senses among the foregoing is in part due to the dual etyma *cuppus* and *cupus;* however it is also apparent that a great amount of overlapping in meaning takes place among the various descendants, hence our inclusion of masc. forms of either type.) The same variety in meaning is apparent in the following: (Sardinia) Campid. *kuppu* 'wine cask', cf *DES*, 1, 434b; as well as on these maps of the *AIS*: 972 'wooden bowl': (W. Rheto-Romance) Sursilvan (P. 1, 3, 10, 11, 13), and other (P. 5, 14, 16, 17), (North) Ven. (P. 307, 330, 340), Pied. (P. 122, 143), Lig. (P. 160, 170, 175, 181); 971 'earthenware basin': (North) Ven. (P. 341), (Central) Lat. (P. 624); 973 'earthenware basin': (North) Lomb. (P. 229), Pied. (P. 117); 1321 'wine vessel': (Central-intersection of Abr.-Umbria-Lat.) (P. 645). Olivieri, 205a, also cites Tuscan *coppo* 'earthenware vessel', while Traina notes a Sicilian form *coppu*, 226a. (We merely note in passing other related meanings apparent in *AIS* 666 'receptacles of various kinds', 970 'bowl for lard', 1523 'wash basin'.)

Dialectally the forms occur in a large area of Italy with the heaviest concentration however in Rhaetia and N. Italy. The notion of basin or bowl is predominant but the uses to which the item may be put are varied (wine, washing, etc.). Given parallel reflexes in a widespread area of W. Romania it would appear likely that the masc. forms were spontaneously and independently derived from *cupa*.

1.4. SUMMARY

Of the six items treated here, *buttis* and *tina* are virtually pan-Romance and hence enjoy extremely frequent attestation. The two derivative forms *butticella* and *cuppus* are much less frequent. Dialectally the former appears only in the north: however it is noteworthy for the fact that it has entered standard Italian, hence forming an etymological couplet with *butticula*. *Cup(p)us* is quite widely attested in W. Romance, including Sardinia, Rhaetia and Italy. The reflexes of *caccabellus* and *cucumella* are exceedingly rare, and are restricted to S. Italy except for one citation of *cucumella* in the Piedmont. The importance of doc. 8 is underlined as it demonstrates the following: 1) that certain items which are now highly restricted in scope *(caccabellus, cucumella)* must have enjoyed earlier far greater currency, 2) that despite the overall conservatism of our collection, in which the scribes generally appear to have been trying to write CL, a number of items, most of which are derived from classical forms, appear for the first time *(butticella, caccabellus, cuppus)* or make their appearance after only one possible previous occurrence each *(cucumella, tina).*

Lastly it is noted that special importance is to be attached to the meanings associated with all of these items. We have shown that *caccabellus* and *cucumella,* in addition to sharing a comparable history of derivation and later attestation, are closely related in sense; in doc. 8 the distinction appears to be largely one of size (i. e., weight). *Buttis* appears in one of the senses normally associated later with it in Romance, i. e., 'barrel'. However, along with *butticella,* it appears as a dry measure, a sense not found later. Furthermore, *tina* differs from the later concept of "vat", etc., in that it is described as being closed. For representations and descriptions of containers and vessels of all sorts, we cite the following in Scheuermeier: (those destined for milk, butter, cheese) 24-28, 29-34, 35-46, (hay) 62-68, (water as in watering cans) 77, (grain storage) 143-144, (various vessels associated with wine, for transporting, pressing, fermenting, etc.) 152-155, 155-159, 160-163, 163-168, 170-172, 172-175, 175-176, (olive oil) 180-193. With specific reference to *botte* and *tina,* cf 170 and 154-155, 160-161. It is apparent that the fundamental distinction between 'storage barrel' and 'fermentation vat' is not present in our collection. Finally we have noted the semantic problems involved in *cup(p)us.*

2.1. FIELDS

Various items, among which *terra* and *campus,* appear in close proximity to one another in the following context in doc. 20 (Ravenna, ca. 600): *cum terris et vineis et omnibus*... (4), and *finibus, terminis, campis, pratis, pascuis, silvis, salectis, sationalibus, vineis*... (11). Both *terra* and *campus* are glossed by Tjäder as "field". Strictly speaking, neither enjoys the sense in CL; *terra* refers to land or earth, while *campus* implies open, plain country. In addition, both items are pan-Romance, the former usually in its classical sense, the latter however as a replacement of CL *ager.* In Italy, *terra* is attested dialectally as 'field', i. e., arable land;

hence we treat here of the geographical repartition of the two items in Italy. (We have noted above the fact that dialectal division in our texts is not pertinent inasmuch as both items appear in doc. 20; compare the like situation involving vessels, etc., in doc. 8.)

a. *campus*

The encroachment of *campus* upon *ager* is generally fixed from the 4th c. on, cf *FEW*, 2, 162a; Corom., 1, 621a; Rohlfs, *Ager*, 9, 59-60; Olivieri, 124b. The process begins sporadically even in CL, cf *ThesLL*, 3, 213, 31. In any event doc. 20 (ca. 600) is antedated by a considerable period. Citations from approximately the same time are: Gregory the Great (ca. 540-604), cf Rohlfs, *Ager*, 9; a text of Childebertus (Frankish king, 596), the *formulae Andecavenses* (Anjou, end of the 6th c.), Niermeyer, 123b; the *Lex Salica* (6th c.), cf Rohlfs, *Ager*, 9-10. Thereafter *campus* predominates, though there are occasional survivals of *ager* in the Romania, see below.

b. *terra*

Terra is equated by Arnaldi with *ager, praedium* in Gregory the Great (ca. 540-604). Otherwise the following citations fall after doc. 20: *Edictus* of Rotharus (Lombardy, 636-652), a text from Cassino (in Campania, 772), the *Codex Cavensis* (Salerno, in Campania; 798), a text from Amalfi (Campania, 860), a text of Berengarius (899), a document from Parma (Emilia, 908), a text from the monastery of S. Silvester in Capite (possibly the same as the monastero di Sant'Andrea al Monte Soratte, near Rome; 955), a text from Bari (Apulia, 977), a document from Sardinia (1002), a document from Conversano (in Apulia), history of the abbey of Cassino (Campania), document from Novi (Genoa, in Liguria; 946-1230), document from Tortona (Piedmont; 913-1358), cf Arnaldi.

It is apparent that the attestations occur in a widespread area in Italy, as well as in Sardinia; there is no clear-cut predominance of north or south. The modern dialectal distribution shows quite another pattern in our examination of the maps of *AIS* 1180 'fertilize the fields', and 1416 'field'. We report here only the totals, first of *campus*, then of *terra*, found in the following regions: Rhaetia: 27:0; North (including Alpine Lombardic): 171:9; Central: 60:4; South: 27:20; Sardinia: 18:2. The total number of attestations results in the ratio 303:35 and it is obvious that *terra* occurs only slightly better than 10 % as often as *campus*. The really striking part of the tabulation is the very consistent increase in the percentage of attestations of *terra* as one goes from north to south. Just as there are no occurrences at all of *terra* in Rheto-Romance, *campus* does not appear in Calabria or Sicily. Sardinia merely follows the overall pattern.

2.2. SOWN

Campus in its later sense of 'field' implies a susceptibility to cultivation; two other items appear in our collection which more specifically state the fact that fields have been or are capable of being sown: *agros arvos* (Syracuse, 10-11; 489), and *sationales* (Ravenna, 20; ca. 600). (It is to be noted immediately that the former may be interpreted either as two nouns, or as a noun and an adjective; we have generally followed the latter interpretation, cf Tjäder's *errata*.) Neither form survives long in Romance, though there are possible reflexes of *arvus* as a noun (see below), and *sationalis* as an adj. (see below). The forms are noteworthy for two reasons, 1) they demonstrate a regional differentiation, and 2) they occur in highly parallel contexts: *omnes fines, terminos, agros arbos, cultos vel incultos, seu vineas* (10-11-4-2), and *finibus, terminis, campis... sationalibus, vineis* (20-11), (see page 57 for the fuller context). It is noted that *campus, terra* and *sationales* all occur in one series of items in doc. 20; in brief, docs. 10-11 and 20 account for all of the interesting items.

c. *ager*

The fact that *ager* is accompanied by *arvus* (as noun or as adjective) is doubtless indicative of the weakening of *ager* in the face of *campus. Ager* and *arvus* are closely associated throughout the literature, as: Plautus (ca. 297, and ca. 292 BC), cf *ThesLL*, 1, 1289, 44; Du Cange, 1, 415c; *ThesLL*, 1, 1282, 51; Cicero (died 43 BC; *agri arvi*), cf *ThesLL*, 2, 731, 34; Varro (47-45 BC), cf

ThesLL, 2, 731, 30; Festus (died ca. AD 150; *arvum dicimus agrum necdum satum*), cf *ThesLL*, 1, 1289, 37; Servius (born 390), cf *ThesLL*, 1, 1289, 25. Later uses are found in Isidore (ca. 560-ca. 640), cf *CGL*, 4, 486, 34; and in Rotharus (Lombardy; mid-7th c.), cf Du Cange, 1, 415c.

Ager survives sporadically in N. Italy *(Codex diplomaticus Longobardorum*), and in S. France in place-names and in legal language, in the 8th and 10th c., cf Rohlfs, *Ager*, 10; *FEW*, 1, 53a. It is specifically equated with *campus* in the *lex Baiuvariorum* (741-744), cf *Mittellat. Wörterb.*, 1:3, 374b, as well as in much later Polish sources (generally Cracow, Plock, Gniezno, Poznan, Vilnius, etc., from the 13th c. until 1519), cf *Słow. łac.*, 354f.

Various reflexes of *ager* appear in early Romance, as follows: old Ven. *agro* (cf *REW*, 276; Rohlfs, *Ager*, 5, 10), old Sard. (Logud.) *agru* (cf *FEW*, 1, 53a; *DES*, 1, 62a; Rohlfs, *Ager*, 5), old Rum. *agru* (cf Körting, 34; Rohlfs, *Ager*, 5, 10), old Prov. *agre* (cf *FEW*, 1, 53a, 'place where wild animals prefer to graze'; Rohlfs, *Ager*, 6), old Bearnais (cf Rohlfs, *Ager*, 10), old Galician *agra* (cf Rohlfs, *Ager*, 5, 10) or *agro* 'enclosed piece of land' (cf *REW*, 276; Morais, 1, 490b). The old Sp., old Port. form *ero* presents a problem with regard to etymon (*ager* or *area*). For a summary of the previous treatments of the word, cf Rohlfs, *Ager*, 4, 5, concerning the views of Cornu, Baist, Michaelis, Körting, Hanssen, and Castro. Both Morais and Corominas consider the form to be a masc. formation of *era* 'piece of terrain on which grain is threshed', derived from CL *area*, while García de Diego, 580b, considers its origin as *ager*. Such forms as the following are cited, *eira* (938), *era* (950), and *eiro* (1018), *ero* (1109), cf Corom., 2, 310a and b; similarly Morais, 4, 218a, and 4, 217b, notes both *eiro* and *eira*. However, though the form may be derived from *area*, Corom. notes, 2, 311a, that the sense of CL *ager* 'field' was likely transferred in certain instances, as Arag. *ero* 'division of a garden', and Ast. *eru*, which has two senses, 'threshing ground' or 'farm, property'. Compare the citation in Morais, 4, 593a, of *ero* in the sense "country estate divided by boundary lines'. The connection with the notion of "tilled field' is noted by Corom.; however he admonishes against speaking of any formal popular survival of *ager* in Spain.

Nonetheless reflexes of *ager* are frequent in Iberia, as: in place-names (cf Rohlfs, *Ager*, 6; Alcover-Moll, 1, 298b), Cat. *agre* (cf Rohlfs, *Ager*, 5, 10; Alcover-Moll, 1, 317a), Gal. *agro*, Port. *agro* (cf Rohlfs, *Ager*, 5, 10; Morais, 1, 490b), and *agra* (Morais, 1, 479a), Mallorcan *agre* (cf *REW*, 276; Alcover-Moll, 1, 317a 'field that bears fruit without cultivation'), Minorcan *agre* (cf Alcover-Moll, 'place where one is born and for which a longing is felt'). In Italy, forms are attested in widely separated regions: Bergamo (Lombardy) *ager, age* (cf *REW; FEW*, 1, 53a; Rohlfs, *Ager*, 5, 10), and Calabria, *agər* (cf *FEW*; Rohlfs, *Ager*, 5). As for Rheto-Romance *er* a problem is posed similar to that in old Sp. and old Port., for a summary of which cf Rohlfs, *Ager*, 5, concerning the views of Ascoli (who derives the form from *agrum*), Gartner, Salvioni and Körting *(area)*, and Meyer-Lübke (either *ager* or *area*). Rohlfs, *Ager*, 7, points out that either is phonologically possible but concludes that the meaning is consistently "sown field". Considerable support is lent to this reasoning by the citations of *AIS* 1416, in which the forms appear in the sense of 'arable land' (P. 1, 3, 5, 10, 11, 13, 14, 15, 16, 17, 19, 25, 27, 28, 47).

It is clear that *ager* was more widely distributed in earlier stages of Romance (old Rum., old Sard., etc.). Nonetheless it makes a strong showing in Iberia and Rhaetia, whereas it appears only sporadically in Italy. While the usage in doc. 10-11 is merely that of CL, it would possibly indicate that the item was at one time even more widespread in Italy, i. e., in Sicily.

d. *arvus*

The adjective *arvus*, 'ploughed, arable' in CL, does not survive in Romance. In view of the possibility that we have to deal with a masc. substantive, *arvus* ←— *arvum*, we note the following: Sard. (Logud.) *arvu* (*REW*, 692; *DEI*, 1, 313a; *DES*, 1, 132a; in which it is also classed as old Logud.; Rohlfs, *Ager*, 5, also old Sard. *Arvum* or *arva* is further possibly attested in the French Ardennes, *arve* '*champ, terrain vide*' (cf *FEW*, 1, 151a); while Godefroy, 1, 416a, also derives old Fr. *arve* '*champ*' (1326) from *arva*.

We have noted above the co-occurrence of *arvus* with *ager*. The noun form *arvum* (or *arvus*) appears in Paulus Diaconus (8th c.), and in a text from Salerno (Campania; before the 10th c.), cf Arnaldi. It is specifically cited by Sleumer, 129b, as belonging to Christian Latin. *Arvum* and *arvus* likewise occur in Polish sources from the late 14th c. through the 15th c. (sample contexts: *agros et arwos; arvos seu campos; agros, campos, arvos*), cf *Słow. łac.*, 802.

e. *sationalis*

We have noted a fair degree of associative use among *campus-ager-arvus*; that the same is true for *sationalis* is confirmed by this citation from Servius (4th c.) and Isidore: *omnia terra... quadrifariam dividitur: aut enim arvus est ager, id est sationalis...*, cf *ThesLL*, 1, 1289, 25; 2, 731, 33. Another early use which appears before doc. 20 occurs in Gregory the Great (ca. 540-604), cf Souter, 365a; Blaise, 740a; Niermeyer, 940a. Subsequent attestations of the form used either adjectivally or as a noun, appear thus: a Saxon text (704), cf Niermeyer, 940a; the *Codex diplomaticus Longobardorum* (772), cf Niermeyer; a text from Nonantula (Emilia, 772), cf Arnaldi, Niermeyer; text from Xanten (Germany, 866-1280; *sacionalem* appears with *ager*), cf *Mittellat. Wörterb.*, 1: 3, 374a; text from the monastery of S. Silvester in Capite (possibly near Rome, see page 58; 955), cf Arnaldi; and a document of the Ravenna Church (10th c.), cf Sella, *GLE*, 301, 137; *terra sacionale*.

The form is preserved in medieval Latin largely in the north; further note the overt connection with Ravenna. As an adjective the item is attested solely in middle French, *sational* 'reserved for sowing" (1540), cf *FEW*, 11, 243a.

2.3. DESERTED

We have made reference above to the importance of the contexts in which various items involving the concept of land occur. In doc. 10-11 (Syracuse, 489), the sequence *agros arbos* is immediately followed by *cultos vel incultos*. Hence it may not be inferred that *cultus* is so much a synonym of *ager arvus* as it is an added qualification in sense, i. e., 'tilled, worked'. Similarly its antonym *incultus* merely means 'not maintained, unworked'. In view of its later rivalry in Italy with *desertus*, we treat both items under the broad category of 'deserted, abandoned'.

f. *desertus*

Desertus, a participial adjective from CL *desero* 'forsake, abandon', appears in doc. 3 (Ravenna, mid-6th c.?) in connection with a *colonia* which has lain abandoned. It is similarly employed by Isidore (XIV, viii, 31) with reference to uncultivated places, cf *ThesLL*, 5, 683, 80. Yet later attestations, between the 9th and 16th centuries, are noted in which the Greek equivalent for 'desolate, lonely, solitary' is glossed by *desertus*, cf *CGL*, 2, 314, 13; 3, 178, 65; 3, 200, 57; 3, 251, 23; 3, 260, 65; 4, 329, 38, and 4, 437, 59. With specific regard to fields, the item appears earlier in the phrases *deserti agri* and *desertum praedium*, in the *Codex Theodosianus* (438), cf Du Cange, 3, 78c. Interestingly, the *agri deserti*, a term applied to neglected lands, is not a feature of the later Germanic codes owing to the fact that land was too eagerly sought to be abandoned, cf Ernst Levy, 112, 124-125, 194-197.

Desertus nonetheless persists in early and modern Romance: old It. (cf *REW*, 2592; see below for modern dialectal distribution), old Fr. '*ravagé, en friche*' (cf *FEW*, 3, 52b; Godefroy, 2, 578b), old Prov. 'abandoned' (cf *FEW*), Rum. 'empty' (cf *REW*; Puşcariu; Cioranescu, 285); Fr. (cf *REW, FEW*); Prov. (cf Mistral, 1, 756a), Sp. 'abandoned, deserted' (cf Corom., 2, 143a; semi-learned), Port. 'uninhabited, solitary, depopulated' (cf *REW; FEW;* Morais, 3, 1026a), Cat. 'deserted, uninhabitable' (cf *REW; FEW;* Alcover-Moll, 4, 249a).

g. *incultus*

As we have indicated above, the real importance of *incultus* lies in its dialectal distribution in Italy as a rival to *desertus*. It is not commonly found in the sources (e. g., *REW*, Niermeyer, Du Cange), presumably on the grounds that it is a learned word, cf *DEI*, 3, 1990b, which treats it as a translation of Greek *ageō̆rgētos*. An early citation in which *desertus* and *incultus* are equated is found in Orosius (Spain, 417-418), cf *ThesLL*, 5, 685, 19.

The following is a summary of *desertus* and *incultus* respectively, in *AIS* 1417 'fallow land': (North) Lomb. (P. 274), Pied. (P. 109, 149, 159), Emilia (P. 446; also cf *REW*, 2592; Puşcariu), Lig. (P. 187), (Central) Tusc. (P. 511); and (North) Ven. (P. 307, 373, 381), Lomb. (P. 270), Pied. (P. 123), Emilia (P. 415), and (Central) Marche (P. 538), Umbria (P. 576). It is evident that both forms are restricted to N. and C. Italy; indeed, we observe that Lombardy, Piedmont, and Emilia are represented by both. Doc. 10-11 indicates that *incultus* was known in this sense in Syracuse but was later preserved in other regions. On the other hand, we note a very likely northern origin for reflexes of *desertus*.

2.4. VINEYARD

In the citations of various contexts which we have made earlier, see pages 57, 59, we have incidentally noted occurrences of *vinea* 'vineyard' (docs. 10-11, Syracuse; 20, Ravenna). Since it is pan-Romance, we do not treat it further, except to note that it is rivalled by the phrase *ortu vineatu* in doc. 17 (Rome, beginning of the 7th c?).

h. *vineatus*

The form first appears in our collection, but is relatively well attested thereafter in N. and C. Italy, as follows: Parma (Emilia, 907), cf Sella, *GLE*, 390; *DEI*, 5, 4052a; Tivoli (Latium, 945 and 954), cf Sella, *GLI*, 160, 393; Rome (1003), cf Sella, *GLI*, 427; Bologna (Emilia, 1105), cf Sella, *GLE*, 320; a text from Farfa (Umbria, 1106-1118), cf Du Cange, 8, 341a; texts from Lombardy (1270, 1284, 1300), cf Bosshard, 106, 304, 82; Piacenza (Emilia, 14th c.), cf Sella, *GLE*, 390, 279; Lombardy (1365), cf Bosshard, 109; Montalboddo (Marche, 1366), cf Sella, *GLI*, 447; Aquila (Abruzzi, 14th c.), cf Sella, *GLI*, 677; Lombardy (1376, and twice in 1461), cf Bosshard, 303, 110, 104. (An additional citation from 1328, unidentifiable as to place of origin, is cited in Du Cange, 8, 341b.)

Although all of the previous citations from Sella are listed under *vineare*, 'to plant with vines', it is apparent that the actual forms are adjectival. The verb form itself appears in Istria (1292), cf Sella, *GLI*, 624; its history is not only much later than the adjectival form but also much less well attested. Both *vignato* and *vignare* have been adopted by standard Italian. The medieval attestations bespeak a C. Italian origin, which soon reached N. Italy as well. We note in passing that *vineatus* is coupled with a number of other forms, e. g., *orticellum, pergola*, etc., however not specifically with *hortus*.

Elsewhere comparable adjective, verb and even noun forms, appear in early Romance; such forms frequently are compounded with *ad-*, as: old Prov. *avinhat* (cf *FEW*, 14, 472b), and *vinhada* 'récolte d'une vigne' (cf *FEW*, 14, 472a, Em. Levy, 8, 782b), old Fr. *vigner* 'cultiver la vigne' (1356; cf *FEW*, 14, 472b), and *avignier* (1245-1393; cf *FEW*, 14, 472b). Compare an occurrence of the compounded verb *invineare* in medieval Latin, from an earlier time, in Gubbio (1124), cf Sella, *GLI*, 297.

Given the late dates of strictly verbal forms not only with regard to Italy but also to France, it appears most probable that the infinitive forms derive from the adjective, and not directly from CL *vinea* or its reflexes.

2.5. SUMMARY

Of the eight items treated, we note but one, *vineatus*, which is apparently first attested in our collection. Six of the remaining are classical items; *sationales* appears in the 4th century. In terms of distribution in the Romania, *campus* and *terra* are pan-Romance; *desertus* is also widespread in occurrence.

The forms referring to sown fields have less staying power; while adjectival *arvus* does not survive, *sationalis* survives (as an adjective) only in middle French. *Ager* is relatively frequent in a variety of locations, especially in Iberia and Rhaetia. With specific reference to Italy, *campus* is far more frequent than *terra* in the sense of 'field'; however the latter becomes proportionately stronger in the south. *Sationales*, which is not found in the modern dialects, is preserved in medieval Latin, mainly in N. Italy. Similarly, the modern reflexes of *desertus* and *incultus*, though relatively infrequent, are found principally in the north. The occurrence of *incultus* in doc. 10-11 may suggest however that the item was at one time more widely distributed in Italy. Finally, *vineatus* is heavily attested throughout the course of its evolution in C. and N. Italy; it not only enters standard Italian but may also be the forerunner of certain old Prov. and old Fr. forms.

Though patterns of dialectal distribution are discerned, the best correlation with our collection is found in the case of *vineatus* and *sationales;* only the former survives in Italy today however.

3.1. Dwellings and Landed Estates

Our texts abound in terms which refer to the concepts of house, farmhouse or farm, landed estate, and collections of such estates. A certain overlapping exists among the terms, with respect 1) to word formation (e. g., *casa-casale*, etc.), 2) meaning (e. g., the various terms for 'estate'), and 3) function (e. g., *casa* as a qualifier of *fundus*).

3.2. House

We note three items which refer to house, *casa, domus,* and non-CL *domucella,* the last of which does not survive in Romance.

a. *casa*

Casa appears in doc. 8 (Ravenna, 564) and 17 (Rome, beginning of the 7th c.?). In the former the CL sense "small house" is retained; in addition, *casa* appears in both texts as a sort of name or qualifier, first of a specific *casa* (*casa, qui appellatur Casa Nova*), then of *fundi* (*fundus Casa Gini*, etc.). A transition is apparent from the concept of a small, humble dwelling to a type of building by which an entire *fundus* may be characterized. For such uses, cf Josephson, 34, and *ThesLL, Onom.,* 2, 222, 74ff. According to Josephson, 40, *casa* refers to the main building of a *fundus, casale* to subsidiary buildings.

Ultimately, of course, *casa* evolves into the almost universal term in Romance for 'house', with the general exception of France where it is rivalled by *mansio* and *hospitale,* cf *FEW,* 2,

452a; 4, 496b; 6, 248a. (French *case* 'lowly hut' is obviously learned.) The main point here however is the fact that it occurs in its original sense as well as in its later sense in which it serves to differentiate the neologism *casale*. The dialectal distribution is treated below.

b. *domus*

Domus is well attested in the following texts, all of which are from Ravenna: 1 (445-446), 13 (553), 8 (564), 14-15 (572), 6 (575), and 21 (625). Two facts are salient: 1) *domus* co-exists with *casa* in doc. 8, and 2) it is much more frequent than *casa* and appears over a considerably longer period of time, despite the fact that it is ultimately largely replaced in the Romania by other forms, cf Bonnet, 577; Körting. *Lat.-Rom. Wörterb.*, 365.

Remnants of the form are cited in earlier stages of Italian, as: old Bergamesque *dom, domo* 'dwelling' (cf *REW*, 2745; *FEW*, 3, 135b; Lorck, 140, who notes a 14th c. gloss of CL *domicilium*); in Guittone d'Arezzo (lived at Arezzo, in Tuscany, also at Florence and Bologna; ca. 1230-1294, cf Monaci, 184), and in two documents from Sardinia (1173, 1212), cf Monaci, 10, 28.

As for regional attestation, the form is restricted in Italy almost exclusively to place-names, as in N. Italy (Piedmont, Lombardy), cf *FEW*, 3, 135b, and C. Italy (Tuscany, Marche), cf *FEW*, Gatto, in *Arch. Rom.*, 2, 226, and also Olivieri, 246a. The situation in Sardinia however is almost completely conservative: in *AIS* 395, seventeen points show *domo,* while only four points have other forms (two of which are *casa*). Further cf *REW*, 2745; *FEW*, 3, 135b; *DES*, 1, 476b; Olivieri.

c. *domucella*

We touch on the non-CL diminutive *domucella* for its bearing on the ultimate change of sense in *casa*. We have noted that it does not survive in Romance. (Compare the fate of *horticellus*, with which it appears in our collection, see page 21.) Its appearance in doc. 25 (Ravenna, 1st half of the 7th c.?), is antedated by a first attestation in the *Peregrinatio* (Spain, 4th c.), cf Souter, 112b; Niermeyer, 354b; *ThesLL*, 5, 1948, 77. Later attestations range over three centuries, and appear throughout Italy: Rome (769), cf Niermeyer; Rome (9th c.), cf Sella, *GLI*, 213; Ravenna (10th c.), cf Sella, *GLE*, 129; Gaeta (Campania, 954), cf Niermeyer; Arnaldi; Sella, *GLI*, 213; Ravenna (1017), cf Arnaldi; Sella, *GLE*, 129.

In consideration of the dates involved, the fact that a diminutive of *domus* was required gives indirect evidence to the fact that *casa* lost its nuance of small, humble home sometime between the middle of the 6th c. (doc. 8, *casa* in classical sense), and the beginning of the 7th c. (25, *domucella;* and 17, *casa* as noun attribute). (Despite the fact that doc. 17 is from Rome, we have shown in the citations that *domucella* was employed there in the 8th and 9th centuries.)

3.3. FARMHOUSE

Colonica and *casalis*, both of which are derivatives of CL forms, appear in our collection in the sense of 'farmhouse'. Dialectally the latter has considerable extension in the Romania, while *colonica* survives only in old French and Swiss French dialects. Both forms occur in our collection in strikingly similar contexts.

d. *colonica*

The substantive *colonica* is derived from the adjective *colonicus*, and arises from association with *mansio*. It appears in the sense of 'farmhouse' in doc. 13 (Ravenna, 553) in the following context: *earum massarum... cum... colonicis subsequentibusque suis, finibus, terminis*, etc. (5-8). The occurrence is preceded only by usage in Ausonius (4th c.), cf *FEW*, 2, 921a; *ThesLL*, 3, 1705, 10. Three senses are associated with the item in the course of its semantic development: holding of a *colonus*, manorial holding or *mansus*, land of a *mansus*. Although the first and last senses are attested from the 5th century, the notion of *mansus* or farmhouse appears considerably later, as: in Ludovicus (814), a text from 819/820 (but not otherwise identified as to place of origin), from the council of Valence (Bas-Dauphiné, 855), cf Niermeyer, 203a.

In the Romania the form appears in old Fr. *colonge* however in the sense of farm, '*fonds de terre concédé à un colon*', cf *FEW*, 2, 921a; Du Cange, 2, 413c; old Neuchâtelois (13-15th c.) and old Bernois (1343), cf *FEW*. Though the item does not survive in Italy, it is found later in a very conservative part of the Romania.

e. *casalis*

Casalis, or *casale*, is a non-CL neologism derived from *casa*. (Compare our previous remarks concerning *runcilio* and *bracile*, see pages 17, 27.) While the function of the item is at first adjectival, 'of a rural dwelling', it later assumes use as a noun, cf Niermeyer, 150a; Souter, 41a; Sleumer, 193a.

It is found in our collection in the following pertinent contexts: doc. 8 (Ravenna, 564) *ex casa... Ravennati territorio... uncias quattuor; ex casale Petroniano territorio Bononiense... uncias duas* (2-15), and doc. 17 (Rome, beginning of the 7th c.?) *massa... cum fundis et casalibus suis* (9-10, 29-30). In the case of the former, we find a series of structures which are listed in declining size: *casa* which, as we have noted on page 66, retains its classical sense of 'humble dwelling'; it is preceded by several instances of *domus* (which we have not cited) in its classical sense 'house'. In the second context *casale* is couple with *fundus* 'farm, rural property"; it will be further noted that there is a parallelism between the citation and that noted earlier for *colonica*, see previous pages. In both instances, *casale* is best treated as 'farmhouse'. Compare our remarks on the relationship between *casa* and *casale* above, page 67. To a certain extent *casale* appears as a continuator of the classical sense of *casa*, however in a specifically rural connotation. Note for example dialectal attestations in N. Italy in the related senses 'small house', cf *FEW*, 2, 455a, and 'rural house in ruins', *DEI*, 1, 788b.

As for the history of the form, it is attested as an adjective in the *gromatici*, cf *REW*, 1729; *FEW*, 2, 455a; *DEI*, 1, 788b; *ThesLL*, 3, 511, 55; Josephson, 38ff. The noun use however appears for the first time in doc. 8 or in other nearly contemporaneous sources, as Gregory the Great (540-604), cf Blaise, 135b; *ThesLL*, 3, 511, 81; and a papyrus from 572, studied by Marini, cf *ThesLL*. Moreover with regard to Rome, doc. 17 appears to show the form first. Attestations which can be situated specifically in Italy are the following: Rome (761), cf Niermeyer, 150a; Spoleto (in Umbria, 773), cf Niermeyer, Arnaldi; Teatino (mod. Chieti, in the Abruzzi; 840), cf Niermeyer; the *Liber pontificalis* (9th c.), cf Sella, *GLI*, 130; Rome (9th c.), cf *DEI*, 1, 788b; Charles III (879), cf Niermeyer; Gaeta (in Campania, 903), cf Niermeyer; Ugo (928), Pope Agapitus (946-955), and Pope Sylvester II (999-1003), cf Arnaldi; from Reggio (in Emilia, before 1050), cf Arnaldi; Rimini (14th c.), cf Sella, *GLE*, 79, 'hamlet'. It is evident that a preponderance of the citations center about Rome, with sporadic attestations in S. and N. Italy. (We merely note in passing the citations in Du Cange, 2, 198c, which are from France from a later period, 1415, etc., and in *Slow. łac.*, 218, Cracow, Poland, 1455-1480).

As for occurrences or reflexes of the form in the Romania, they are very widespread, especially in W. Romance, but also in Vegliote, However the specific sense of 'farmhouse' is but one of many associated with the item. The following pertinent senses are cited in early Romance: old Fr. 'farm', 'dairy', 'manor surrounded by fields ready for cultivation', (cf Godefroy, 2, 107a; *REW*, 1729; *FEW*, 2, 454a), old Prov. 'small house' or 'garden or enclosure surrounding a house' (cf *FEW*, 2, 454a, also 2, 454b, 'old house in ruins'). The situation in modern Romance is the following: Prov. 'rustic house', 'garden which surrounds a house' (cf *REW*, 1729; Mistral, 1, 483a), Sp. 'rustic house' (cf *REW*; Corom., 1, 713b, also 'ruins, place which had been inhabited', 'manorial house'), Cat. 'rustic building' (cf *REW;* Alcover-Moll, 3, 9b), Port. 'rustic house or property' (cf *REW;* Morais, 2, 984b). The situation in Swiss French dialects is less well defined. Of the many senses attributed to the Swiss French form, that of 'outbuilding' is one of the least certain, cf *Gloss. des pat. de la SR*, 3, 518b and 519b. As for Rumanian, Cioranescu, 146, cites a form *casaba*, accompanied by an alternate form ending in *-ale*, 'town, village'. The first form is doubtless derived from Turkish *kasaba* (compare Arabic *kasaba* 'fortress', cf *FEW*, 2, 453b). However, given the sense of 'town', which as we shall point out subsequently is attested in Italy for *casale*, it seems most probable that the Rum. forms are the result of a chance etymological coincidence in two different languages.

STUDIES IN ROMANCE LEXICOLOGY 71

In place-names the item is frequent in France, cf Vincent, 278-279; Italy, cf *DEI*, 1, 788b, Olivieri, 33a and 147a; and Switzerland (very heavy attestation), cf *Gloss. des pat. de la SR*, 3, 518b.

Strictly speaking, the sense 'farmhouse' is not found in Italy except in the related senses which we cited above for N. Italy, 'small house', etc., cf *DEI*, 1, 788b. As for the rest of Italy, the sense evolves from the notion of an isolated rural building to that of the 'hamlet', i. e., an assemblage of such units. This sense is noted as follows in *AIS* 818: (Central) Latium (two points, including Rome), and (South) Campania (three points), Sicily (one point, cf also Traina, 172a). (*AIS* 817 'village' similarly shows usage in the south, at one point each in Calabria and Sicily.)

Two patterns of geographical correlation emerge from our study. First, we have shown a relationship which commences with doc. 17 in Rome, and which is continued in the medieval Latin attestations principally in C. Italy, and which ultimately appears dialectally in C. and S. Italy in the evolved sense of 'hamlet'. As for doc. 8, which originates in Ravenna, the fundamental sense of 'farmhouse' is continued not only in certain N. It. dialectal forms, but also in the general W. Romance area (old Fr., Prov., Sp., Port.), cf Josephson, 43. The Rumanian variant possibly shows a development parallel to that for Italy in general.

3.4. ESTATE

Four items appear in our collection which may be classed under the notion of 'estate', *colonia, fundus, praedium,* and *massa*. We shall treat the first three only briefly; *colonia* and *praedium* survive in Romance only in learned form; *fundus* is widespread but in different senses. Of greatest interest is *massa* which assumes a specialized sense of patrimony or group of estates, which is continued alone in Italy.

f. *fundus*

Fundus appears frequently in our collection, including the earliest (1; 445-446) as well as the latest Ravenna text (23; ca.

700?). Among the NR texts it occurs in 10-11 (Syracuse, 489), and 17 (Rome, beginning of the 7th c. ?). It survives in standard Italian in the compound *latifundo* 'vast country estate'. In *AIS* 1180, reflexes of the form are attested in the sense of 'field', which of course is inappropriate for our purposes.

g. *praedium*

A fair degree of interchangeability is noted between *fundus* and *praedium* in medieval Latin glosses, as: *fundi praedia: campi*, and in another sense, *praedia fundi: villae* (document of St. Gallen, 9th-13th c.), cf *CGL*, 4, 240, 20; 4, 269, 18. Legal distinctions arise in regard to its use in medieval Latin, as 1) 'a real estate held in full ownership in contradistinction to tenancies', 2) 'land subject to the supreme proprietary right of a feudal lord', and 3) 'real estate', cf Niermeyer, 830a. The item is adopted as a learned form in standard It., *predio* '*podere, possesso di terra*', cf *DEI*, 4, 3056b.

In comparison with *fundus*, *praedium* occurs somewhat less frequently in our collection, in Ravenna documents 8 (564) and 14-15 (572), and in NR texts, 10-11 (Syracuse, 489), and 18-19 (Rome, beginning of the 7th c. ?). It is noted that both *fundus* and *praedium* appear in docs. 8 and 10-11. A general distinction between the two lies in the fact that *fundus* is frequently qualified by a name or other designation which implies a specific estate. However, *praedium* also appears in the sense of country estate (e. g., 10-11-3-12), as well as a general term for goods or property (e. g., 10-11-3-6, etc., and 18-19-30, etc.). Comparison of the following citations further demonstrates the practical equatability of the two items: *praedia rustica* (8-2-14), *rusticis urbanisque praediis* (14-15-1-11), and *fundum rusticum seu urbanum* (Rome, 1398), cf Sella, *GLI*, 255. With regard to the survival of *fundus* in place-names in Italy and France, cf Olivieri, 307a.

h. *colonia*

The item appears frequently (in abbreviated form) in doc. 3 (Ravenna, mid-6th c. ?), and once in doc. 2 (Ravenna, 565-570). The latter instance is noteworthy for the fact that *coloniae* is coupled with *fundi*, both of which are subservient to a *patrimo-*

nium, which we treat incidentally in the ensuing discussion. *Colonia* is equated specifically with *fundus* and *praedium* in *Słow. łac.*, 613 (Poland, 1532). The term survives in Romance as a learned form, cf *FEW*, 2, 920b; *DEI*, 2, 1019b; and as a place-name, cf *FEW*.

i. *massa*

Massa, in CL 'lump or mass of bread dough', undergoes considerable extension in sense in late and medieval Latin to comprehend, among many others, the concepts of 'estate' and especially of 'patrimony or collection of estates or goods'. Although the implications of the term vary according to the nature of the objects referred to, the dominating notion is that of a 'mass' of several things constituting a certain unity, cf *Diz. encicl. it.*, 7, 473a, and Olivieri, 432b.

In Italy, the term assumes a legal connotation: "Nel diritto romano si adopera il termine 'massa' per indicare un complesso di più cose, che formano una certa unità; di qui probabilmente derivò la denominazione data a grandi possessi dell'alto Medioevo", cf *Enc. it.*, 22, 503a. Strecker, 52, and Habel, 235, both give the related sense of 'administrative district'.

The institution appears relatively frequently in our collection, in the following chronological order: 1 (Ravenna, 445-446), 10-11 (Syracuse, 489), 13 (553), 2 (565-570), and 17 (Rome, beginning of the 7th c. ?). Inasmuch as the references in doc. 1 are also to *massae* in Sicily, the importance of the attestations in the NR-texts is particularly striking. With specific reference to the constitution of the Sicilian estates mentioned in docs. 1, 10-11 they are described as 'riunione dei beni... chiamate *massae*', which were cultivated by slaves or *coloni*, and administered by *actores* and *conductores*, cf Pace, 4, 225-226, 228. Hence, in partial summation, the concept is thus defined: '*ensemble de biens et de droits, d'où propriété, administration*' (Blatt, 239), '*conglobatio ac collectio quaedam possessionum ac praediorum*' (Du Cange, 5, 296b), and 'a more or less compact group of estates held or left behind by an important proprietor' (Niermeyer, 659a). Hence the following definitions are inappropriate: '*fundus cum casa, praedium*' (*ThesLL*,

8, 430, 73), 'estate with dwelling house' (Souter, 244a), and *'indefinitus agrorum modus'* (Arnaldi). (However we hasten to point out that, despite the inexactitude of these definitions, certain of the citations apply to the definition of patrimony, see below.) We have had occasion in our individual discussions of *fundus, praedium,* and *colonia* to note a degree of synonymity among them (see pages 71ff); the following is a functional definition of *massa*, as seen by its relationship with such words as they appear in our collection: 1) *massa* is equatable with *patrimonium* in docs. 1, and 2; 2) it is comprised variously of *fundi* (docs. 1, 10-11, 2, 17), *praedia* (10-11), and *coloniae* (2).

With regard to delineating the semantic history of *massa*, insofar as our collection is concerned, we encounter a problem in that most of our sources do not make a distinction between an 'estate' and a 'patrimony'. As we have intimated above this is particularly serious in the case of the *ThesLL*. Secondly, even those sources which are aware of the distinction may nonetheless include among the examples citations which are more appropriate to yet another idea which has been incorporated into the definition. Hence certain of the citations in Du Cange apply to the definition *'certus agrorum modus'*. Lastly, those sources which maintain the distinction do not necessarily agree with one another in individual cases. Niermeyer in particular is at variance with certain of the other works. Hence we have sought insofar as we were able to list those citations found in more than one source (we note incidentally those instances in which one scholar considers the sense more akin to 'estate' than to 'patrimony').

Docs. 1 (445-446) and 10-11 (489) are among the first instances in which the new sense 'patrimony' appears. Other possible early sources may be seen in Symacchus (384-385), Ammianus Marcellinus (390), *Novellae* of Anthemius (438-468), and the *Donatio Tiburtina* (Tivoli, 471); however they are all cited in Souter, 244a, or *ThesLL*, 8, 430, 73ff, and hence doubtless mean 'estate'. (Also cf *FEW*, 6, 453a, which dates *massa* 'estate' from 384.) Despite the doubtful nature of these citations, one certain early example occurs in the *CIL*, XIV, 3482, 5 (4th c.): *in prediis suis masse Mandelane,* cf Tjäder, 398. Attestations posterior to doc. 10-11 are the following: Cassiodorus (477-570), cf Niermeyer, 659a; Blaise,

517b; *ThesLL*, 8, 430, 79; Gellasius (492-496), cf Niermeyer; Pace, 225-226; Gregory the Great (580-604), cf Niermeyer; Blaise; Du Cange, 5, 296b; *ThesLL*, 8, 430, 81; Farfa (in Umbria, 740), cf *Enc. it.*, 22, 503a; Pope Zacharias (before 752), cf Du Cange; Niermeyer, 'estate'; Pope Hadrianus I (774), cf Blaise; Arnaldi and Niermeyer, 'estate'; a document from Ravenna (904), cf Du Cange; Otto II (977), cf Blatt, 239-240; Niermeyer, 'estate'; Petrus Damianus (1007-1072), cf Du Cange; Henricus III (1040), cf Du Cange; Pope Hadrianus IV (born in England; 1137-1159), cf Blatt; Vincentius Kadłubek (Poland, mid-12th c. to 1223), cf Blatt. As may be seen from the foregoing there is a decided emphasis on Roman attestations. According to the *Enc. it.*, 22, 503a, *massa* came to be applied to possessions of the Roman Church from the 8th c. on. That this had been a practice for probably a century before is shown by doc. 17 (beginning of the 7th c. ?).

As for the Romania, the item is not known in the sense of 'estate' or 'patrimony' outside of Italy, cf *REW*, 5396; *DEI*, 3, 2383b, which cites the usage in 1301-1303 in the sense *'insiemi di beni'*. What is surprising, in view of the frequency of references in our texts to Sicily and to Ravenna, is to find virtually no mention in the medieval citations. The only indirect evidence which we have today of a more considerable prior geographical extent is in place names, as: Massa Fiscaglia (Emilia), M- Lombarda (Emilia, between Ravenna and Bologna), as well as others in C. and S. It. (Massa, the capital of the province Massa e Carrara, Massa Marittima, M- Martana, M- d'Albe, M- di Somma, M- Verona or Trabaria, M- Fermana, etc.) (For additional place-names, cf Olivieri, 432b, and Sleumer, 505b.)

3.5. SUMMARY

We have noted that none of the items which concern us here occurs formally in our collection for the first time. *Casa, domus, fundus, praedium, colonia,* and *massa* are all of course classical forms; *domucella, colonica,* and *casalis* are derived from classical items. The interesting aspects of the items are their evolution in sense and their possible survival in Romance. *Casa* undergoes amelioration in sense, which fact is partially corroborated by the appearance of a form such as *domucella*. However *domucella* does not survive in Romance; *domus*, which is largely replaced by *casa* in the Romania, nonetheless appears later in N. Italy and Sardinia, as well as in toponomastic terms. We have demonstrated that *casa* and *domus* are not employed in our collection as synonyms. In contrast, *colonica* and *casalis,* both of which are adjectival in origin, are virtuously synonymous in the collection. With reference to first attestation, doc. 8 represents one of the first occurrences of *casalis* in a noun function. *Colonica* survives in the Romania on a very limited basis (old Fr., and sporadically in Switzerland), while *casalis* follows two trends: it continues those senses related to 'farmhouse' in W. Romance (N. It., old Fr., etc.), whereas in C. and S. Italy it evolves into the sense 'hamlet'. *Fundus* and *praedium* are quite interchangeable with each other in our collection; *fundus* is widely found in Romance, however, in different senses from that of 'estate'; *praedium* and *colonia* survive only as learned forms. Finally, *massa* undergoes an extensive semantic evolution which is unique to Italy. Our collection represents some of the first attestations of the sense 'patrimony'. Though the usage apparently commences with reference to Sicily and is later prevalent in our Ravenna texts, modern traces of the item are confined in N. Italy to place-names.

4. CHURCH: *ecclesia, basilica*

Two items vie with each other in designating churches: *ecclesia* and *basilica*. As we should expect, the former is by far the more frequent. It appears no fewer than eighty-eight times in our collection; among the Ravenna texts it spans the period between doc. 1 (445-446) and doc. 24 (mid. -7th c.), while in the NR-texts it is found in 17 and 18-19 (both Rome, beginning of the 7th c. ?). However, in all of these texts, with the exclusion of one, *ecclesia* designates the Ravenna church; in doc. 17, it refers to the Church at Rome. *Basilica,* in contrast, occurs in merely two texts, 8 (Ravenna, 564), and Roman 17. It is evident that *basilica* is never employed with reference to the Church as an institution of faith, but rather refers to a specific edifice. In the case of doc. 8, this building is the *basilica sancti Victoris,* while in 17 it is the *basilica sanctae Dei genetricis* (*Mariae*) or the *basilica sancti Petri*. See also Jud, 10, on the use of *basilica* for a memorial church. In the Romania, *ecclesia* is the usual designation for church (although reflexes of *basilica* occur in Vegliote and Rumanian). In certain of the dialects of N. Italy and Grisons (Switzerland), *basilica* is especially noted in this sense, as: old Ven., cf *REW*, 972; Grisons, cf *REW; DRG,* 2, 228a; *AIS* 783 (P. 1, 3, 5, 7, 9, 10, 11, 13, 15, 16, 17, 19, 25, 27, 28, 29, 35, 45, 46, 47). In summary, it is apparent that our collection does not actually demonstrate interchange between *ecclesia* and *basilica;* the terms refer to two different things.

5. DAY: *dies, feria*

Dies, the classical term for 'day', appears very frequently, fifty-four times in all, in both the Ravenna and NR texts. The attestations range from the wills of 4-5 (474-552) to doc. 23 (beginning of the 8th c. ?), and occur in all of the NR texts, 10-11 (Syracuse, 489), 7 (Rieti, 557), and 17 and 18-19 (Rome, beginning of the 7th c.?). In doc. 22 (Ravenna, 639), *feria* and *dies* occur side by side in the following context: *in mense Nobembrio..., octava die, secunda firia...* (61), which was translated by Tjäder, 367, as 'on the eighth day, the second weekday'. Hence it would appear that we have here an instance of a phenomenon which is unusual in our collection: namely, the presence of two lexical items which to all intents and purposes may be considered nearly synonymous. (We have mentioned earlier, with regard to the vessels and containers in doc. 8, the avoidance of synonyms and the fact that items which were quite evidently related always retained a certain individuality.) Despite this, it was our earlier belief that possibly *feria* was not merely a repetition of *dies* but instead represented a sense as yet unattested elsewhere. We shall take up in detail the various points behind our earlier reasoning, pointing out finally our acceptance of Tjäder's translation.

The classical form *feriae* 'holiday' is taken over in the sing. in Christian Latin in the sense of 'weekday'. It is thus observed that the two senses are practically contrary to each other, cf *FEW*, 5, 455b, Paiva Boléo, 7f, and von Wartburg, "*Los nombres*", 5, nt. 1 (concerning a later usage in Portuguese). The following outlines a history of attestations which commences long before the composition of doc. 22 (639); the citations are derived in the main from *ThesLL*, 6, 508, 18ff, and Blaise, 348a, unless otherwise indicated: Tertullian (after 202), also cf Du Cange, 3, 437a; *FEW*, 5, 455b; Bruppacher, 25, 29, 40; Paiva Boléo, 7, nt. 2, von Wartburg, "*Los nombres*", 5; Irenaeus (2nd-3rd c.); the *Peregrinatio* (ca. 383), also cf Lewy, 79-80; Bruppacher, 27; the *Collectio Avellana* (367-553), also cf Bruppacher, 27; Ambrosius (bishop of Milan; 379-397); St. Augustine (386-429), also cf Bruppacher, 22, 23, 25; *FEW*, 5, 452b; von Wartburg, "*Los nombres*", 4; *Cursus Paschalis Victori* (457), cf Bruppacher, 22, 24, 25, 27; Maximus Taurinensis (bishop of Turin; before ca. 465); Uranius (5th c.), also cf Bruppacher, 27; Caesarius Arelatensis (bishop of Arles; died 543), also cf Souter, 146a; von Wartburg, "*Los nombres*", 4; Rohlfs, "*Die Lexikalische*", 27; Isidore, V, xxx, 9 (570-636), also cf *FEW*, 5, 453b; Bruppacher, 22, 25; von Wartburg, "*Los nombres*", 7; Gregory the Great (593), also cf Bruppacher, 29; *regula* of St. Benedict (6th c.); *CIL* (IX, 6150, Brindisi, in Apulia, 6th c.; and X, 4630, Cubulteria, in Campania, 559), cf Bruppacher, 29; *FEW*, 5, 455b. Later attestations are noted in the *Ordo Romanus I* (end of the 7th c.), cf Blaise, 348a; Bede (England, before 735), cf Du Cange, 3, 436c; Gundermann, in *Zeit. f. deutsche Wortforsch.*, 1, 186; Liutprandus (bishop of Cremona, ca. 968), cf Arnaldi; Joanne de Janua (Genoa, 1286), cf Du Cange, 3, 437a; etc.

The usage in late Latin is representative of merely one of three competing systems for designating the days of the week: 1) (Judaic) *una (prima) sabbati, secunda, tertia, quarta,* or *quinta + sabbati, parasceve,* and *sabbatum;* 2) (pagan planetary system) *dies + Solis, Lunae, Martis, Mercurii, Iovis, Veneris* or *Saturni;* and 3) (Christian) *dies dominica* (rarely *feria prima*), *feria + secunda, tertia,* etc., and *sabbatum* (rarely *feria septima*), cf Bruppacher, 6-7; *FEW*, 5, 451b; von Wartburg, "*Los nombres*", 3ff; Hakamies, 71a; Olivieri, 292b; Schmid, 97a; Sleumer, 331a; Strecker, 51; Paiva Boléo, 9. In most of the Romania, with the exception of those regions indicated below, the heathen system prevailed; however in the following typical Romance pattern all three systems are represented: *dominicus dies* (Christian), *lunae dies*, etc. (pagan), and *sabbati dies* (Judaic), cf Bruppacher, 6, 35; Hakamies.

The subsequent uses of reflexes of *feria(e)* in the Romania may thus be regarded as a subsidiary outgrowth of the Christian system, cf von Wartburg, "*Los nombres*", 4. However the reasons for the original adoption of *feria* are not completely clear, cf Bruppacher, 41. Two theories have been advanced both of which center about the fact that the Hebraic term *sabbatum* meant either 'day of rest' or 'week', cf *FEW*, 5, 451b, and ff; Lewy, 78; Bruppacher, 35ff. According to the first theory, *feria* is employed in place of *feriarum*, which would be the equivalent of *sabbati* in the sense of 'rest'; hence, *secunda sabbati*→ *secunda feriarum→ *secunda feria*, cf Gundermann, in *Zeit. f. deutsche Wortforsch.*, 1, 186. The second notion is based upon the fact that the weeks before and after Easter, which were times of rest and fasting among the Christians, were designated *feria secunda*, etc.; subsequently these terms for the weeks about Easter were applied to individual days, cf Du Cange, 3, 436-437, and Paiva Boléo, 8.

Reflexes of the form are virtually pan-Romance, however not in the sense of 'weekday', which is found most notably in Port., cf *REW*, 3250; *FEW*, 5, 452b, and 455b; 3, 464a; Morais, 5, 140b, and 9, 992a; Corom., 2, 511a. Compounds are further noted in N. Italy, as Pied. and Lomb. *feraost* (cf *REW*, 3250, Olivieri 292b), Emil. *feragost* (cf *REW*, Olivieri), as well as standard Italian *ferragosto* 'the first day of August' (cf *REW; DEI*, 3, 1622a; Olivieri, 292b). In our original study we also cited sporadic instances in W. Rheto-Romance (Engadine and Sursilvan), on the basis of references in Bruppacher, 41, and *FEW*, 3, 464b. Upon examination, however, of the original source, Jud, 34, nt. 1, it became clear to us that the forms *firer* and *firó* in reality mean 'holiday' and hence are not pertinent to our study.

As we intimated above, our doc. 22 offers a possible problem in the interpretation of the exact function and meaning of *feria*. We point out that, on the face of it, the phrase *secunda firia* taken by itself would normally be assumed to designate 'Monday'. As such it would correspond not only to the Judaic *secunda sabbati* but also to the later Port. *segunda feira;* it is further undeniable that the sources agree unanimously that the phrase as employed in Christian Latin always indicated 'Monday', cf Niermeyer, 417b; *FEW*, 5, 451b; Bruppacher, 22. Indeed, certain of our citations of *feria* above appear in the phrase, i. e., with *secunda* (e. g., *Cursus Paschalis Victori*, St. Augustine, Isidore).

A possible discrepancy arises however with regard to the companion phrase *octava die*, for it may be pointed out that it is generally glossed as 'Sunday', as in Isidore, VI, xviii, 21 *(octavus dies)*, cf Bruppacher, 15; and Tertullian, cf Blaise, 270a.

The question hence arose as to whether we actually had an instance of *feria* employed merely as a weekday—or in an entirely new sense. Since our text appears long after (7th c.) the first use (3rd c.), the chronology would argue for merely one more example of a usage long since established. But in light of the fuller context of the document, we summarize here the following interpretations which suggested themselves to us: 1) while the 'eighth day' refers to Sunday, *firia* relates to one of the holy *weeks* (note Du Cange's explanation above); this is doubtless to be rejected inasmuch as the month is November; 2) *octava* (or *octavus*) *dies* at one time undergoes a change in sense from 'Sunday' to 'Monday'; however note the use in both Tertullian and Isidore of *octavus dies* as 'Sunday' and *secunda feria* as 'Monday'; 3) *octava dies* still refers to Sunday, but *secunda feria* is employed in the sense of the 'second Sunday' of the month.

The last explanation seemed satisfying to us in that the entire sequence of time indications undergoes apparently a gradation from the general to the particular: i. e., from November to a Sunday, which is further specified as the second Sunday of the month of November. From a semantic point of view, too, the solution had much to recommend it, especially in terms of possible development from the classical sense. Accordingly, the scribe of doc. 22 would have merely taken a CL plural form which enjoyed the sense of 'holiday', reduced it to the singular and applied it to one particular 'holy' day.

Our original conclusion hence was that the usage was a religious one which was however atypical of the more common Christian use. It appeared that the scribe had independently used a form, common to much of late Latin, in a sense which was actually closer to CL. Since such a sense is unattested elsewhere in late Latin as well as in later Romance usage, we were necessarily obliged to conclude that the usage was peculiar to a given scribe.

This uniqueness of attestation of course was enough to occasion some doubt concerning our interpretation. Given our preoccupation with lexical items lifted from context or at best seen in a limited phrasing, it occurred to us subsequently that it should be possible to determine what day in history *secunda firia* had referred to. To be sure, Tjäder, 358, and 362, nt. 2, had given the year 639, while the document itself supplied the month of November, the eighth day *(die)*, and the second *firia* (see earlier for the actual context). The question hence was one of ascertaining exactly what day of the week November 8th, 639 was. Accordingly we had recourse to Giry, who notes (187) that year 639 is designated by the "dominical letter" C, from whose table (246) we learned that indeed November 8th was a Monday!

The obvious question then arose as to what the role of *octava die* might be, and that given its use in the attestations as either Sunday or Monday did it merit investigation. Upon reflection we reached the conclusion that we doubtless had been reading too much into what may be—*but is not necessarily*— a fixed phrase. In other words, while in terms of a *week octava die* may be construed as a specific day, normally Sunday, in terms of the *month* it simply means that it was the eighth day of the 30 or so possible. Finally, it struck us as improbable in any event that such a business transaction (the giving of a donation) should have taken place on a Sunday. Even if this were possible the evidence for *secunda firia* as 'Monday' is overwhelming.

With reference to words for 'weekday' in the contemporary Romania, it could be allowed that some geographical connection exists between the compounds of N. Italy and our text written in Ravenna. However, such a view must be tempered by a realization of the fact that a very lengthy time lapse exists between the first use of *feria* in the sense of 'weekday' and our text (some four centuries). Our text, on the other hand, is highly interesting for the fact that we have an instance of two words, *dies* and *feria*, which are as nearly synonymous as any comparable couplet of words found in our collection. Nonetheless it must be still pointed out that actual identity of meaning never does really occur, as *dies* remains the more general 'day' of the month, *feria* (when qualified by an ordinal number) the more specific 'weekday'.

As for the modern form in Portuguese, it is impossible to trace any direct connection with an attestation from Ravenna in the 7th century. If there ever was a more widespread Romance use of *feria*, it is interesting to note with what thoroughness *dies*, or compounds based upon it (*veneris dies*, etc.) prevailed in the Romania to designate specific days of the week. For a treatment of the geographical distribution of Romance forms for a weekday (specifically 'Friday'), cf Rohlfs, "*Die Lexikalische*", the significance of which is: 1) the only forms which rival *dies* occur in a very limited area (Portugal, *sexta feria*, and part of Sardinia, *cena pura*) (26ff, and map N.º 17), and 2) the frequent correspondence between forms within Iberia, or even between Iberia and Dacia (Rumania), does not hold here (87). (For the concept of a four-membered Romania, namely Iberia, Gallia, Italia, Dacia, cf M. Bartoli, *Caratteri fondamentali della lingua nazionale italiana e delle lingue sorelle*, in *Miscellanea della Facoltà di Letteratura e Filosofia della Reale Università di Torino*, Series I, Turin, 1936, 69-106, and *Caratteri fondamentali delle lingue neolatine*, in *AGl*, 28, 1936, 97-133.) Lastly we point out that only Port. is conservative enough to retain the Christian system for designating days of the week (cf Paiva Boléo, 21); elsewhere, with the rare exceptions of *cena* in part of Sardinia and derivatives of *feria* in N. Italy and standard Italian, it is *dies* and the pagan system which prevails (cf Rohlfs, "*Die Lexikalische*", 27f). Our doc. 22 however employs two of the three forms which are destined ultimately to prevail in sharply defined areas of the Romania.

E. CONCLUSIONS

In the foregoing treatment of the lexicon we have examined in detail approximately forty items, while touching incidentally on several more forms which offer some feature of comparison (*aegritudo, dies, ecclesia, falx, laena, necesse, patrimonium, sata-*

rium, scrinium, testis, and *vinea).* The ensuing resume is developed about four major themes: 1) the items as forms, 2) the semantic development, 3) the attestations of the items in time and in space, and 4) contributions which our study has made to Romance linguistics. For ease of identification, we list here those texts which are pertinent to the summary: (*origin is N. Italy:* Ravenna) 1 (445-446), 4-5: 4th W (474), Concl. portion (552), 13 (553), 3 (mid-6th c. ?), 8 (564), 2 (565-570), 6 (575), 20 (ca. 600?), 16 (ca. 600?), 25 (ca. 600), 21 (625), 22 (639); (*C. It.:* Rome) 17 and 18-19 (beginning of the 7th c. ?); (*S. It.:* Syracuse) 10-11 (489).

1. *Form.* Of the various items studied, by far the greatest number refer to persons, things or institutions. Adjectives form the next largest grouping (*arvus,* 10-11, *necessus,* 17, as well as *desertus,* 3, and *incultus,* 10-11), but several assume the appearance or function of other form classes (verbal *vineatus,* 17, and substantivals: *casalis,* 8, 17, *colonica,* 13, *mansionarius,* 17, *sationales,* 20, and possibly even *arvus,* pages 61f). (*Sarica,* 8, is related to a CL noun which is adjectival in origin.) There is only one function word, *cata,* 6.

The items are classed with regard to origin, according as they are loans from other languages (Greek *cata,* 6, and Gothic or Greek *punga,* 8, and possibly a substratum language in the case of *soca,* 8), derivatives of classical forms, or classical items which undergo a semantic evolution. By far the commonest process of derivation is that of affixation, especially of the diminutive suffixes *-ellus, -cellus: butticella,* 8, *caccabellus,* 8, *domucella,* 25, *horticellus,* 21, 25, *sagellum,* 8, and also *cucumella,* 8, attested once in CL. Other suffixes are *-ilis, -alis* (normally associated with adjectives but used exclusively here with nouns, in *bracile,* 8, possibly *runcilio,* 8, see page 17, and *casalis,* 8, 17, and *sationalis,* 20), *-arius* (in *mansionarius,* 17, and *spatharius,* 16) *-icius (capsicio,* 8), and *-eatus (vineatus,* 17). *Necessus,* 17, represents either an analogical formation or an archaism, while *cup(p)us,* 8, exemplifies change of declension.

It is thus far observed that affixation of *-(c)ellus* is highly frequent in the collection; it is especially common in doc. 8 which accounts for four out of the six forms cited. For surveys of the ending, especially in comparison with another diminutive

-*ittus* in N. Italy, cf Hasselrot, 225-226; and also Rohlfs, *Hist. Gramm.*, 3, 292-293, 350

The same predominance of doc. 8 is further noted in the various other derivatives, of which it accounts for five of the nine examples. Its closest rival with regard to the items of interest thus far cited is Roman 17. We have further indicated that loans play a very small role in our total stock of lexical items. On the contrary, we find that a large number of our items are closely related to forms which also appear in our collection; hence we note the following couplets: *braca-bracile* (both in 8), *buttis-butticella* (both in 8), *casa-casale* (both in 8 and 17), *colonia* (3) -*colonica* (13), *domus* (frequent) -*domucella* (25), *hortus* (17) -*horticellus* (25, 21), *satarium* (?) (8) -*sationales* (20), and *vinea* (20, 10-11) -*vineatus* (17). The same pre-eminence of docs. 8 and 17 is also observable here; we note in passing that *domucella* and *horticellus* appear together in doc. 25.

For the most part the items in our study offer few orthographical peculiarities, with the exception of *caccavello, cuppo, sarica,* and *soca* (all in 8), and to a lesser degree, *firia* (22), *necessae* (10-11), and *tedio* (1). We have noted in *sarica* a possible lexical explanation also (contamination, see page 47).

Finally we point out with regard to Romance reflexes that certain of our items may undergo a morphological change (e. g., *testimonium* in Fr., Sp., Port., pages 46f), or often appear in compounded form (*cata* in S. It., see page 22, *feria* in N. It. dialects and standard It., see page 79, and *vineatus* in old Fr. and old Prov., see page 65.)

2. *Meaning.* Generally those items which are introduced into our collection from non-Latin sources (*cata, punga, soca*) offer no unusual semantic changes; ultimately however the reflexes of *punga* assume a variety of meanings which nonetheless derive from the fundamental notion of 'bag', 'pouch', etc., see page 25. Derivatives of CL forms or those LL forms which change in function necessarily undergo evolution in sense, as the various affixed forms noted above (e. g., *butticella* 'small *buttis*', etc.), or those which are originally adjectival (*casalis* 'of a rural dwelling'→ 'farmhouse', *colonicus* 'pertaining to agriculture'→ *colonica* 'farmhouse', *mansionarius* 'belonging to a dwelling' → 'church servant', and

sationalis 'pertaining to sowing' → *sationales* 'sown fields'). It is noted that *capsicius* doubtless does not yet mean 'window-frame', etc., but is closer to CL *capsa* 'chest', see page 15.

It is especially in CL (or occasionally LL) items that the interesting semantic changes take place. Such evolutions take the following directions: a) extensions in sense, i. e., those effected by the changing requirements of society (*mansionarius, notarius* 'short-hand writer' → 'scribe, secretary'), by the personalization of a word (*potestas* 'power' → 'prefect of a city', *testimonium* 'testimony' → 'witness'), and augmentation or amelioration (*armarium* 'closet' → 'archive, library', *casa* 'small, humble hut' → designation of a *fundus*), and b) restriction or specialization (*statio* 'standing still' → 'place of business', *sarica* 'silk cloth' → 'kind of tunic'). Ultimately a form may undergo both extension and restriction, as *notarius* (noted above) → 'church or royal secretary', and *taedium* 'irksomeness' → 'illness', and finally in Galician a specialized disease peculiar to sheep. We further note two classes of words, those which appear in both a classical and an evolved sense (*armarium* 'cupboard', 8, 'archive, library', 22, and *potestas* 'power', 13, 20, 'office of the praetorian prefect', 16, 'praetorian prefect', 4-5: 4th W & Concl. portion, 2), and those which appear as synonyms of more usual CL terms (*testimonium* 'witness', 1 vs. frequent use of *testis,* and *taedium* 'illness', 1 vs. *aegritudo*, 4-5: 6th W). It is observed that the new sense of *armarium* is chronologically later; however, both *testimonium* and *taedium* appear in our very earliest text and thus antedate the use of the classical terms (*testis, aegritudo*) by considerable periods. To this limited degree, doc. 1 is innovating.

As was the case in word formation, we note a considerable number of couplets or groups of items which may be further classed according as they represent synonymity ('farmhouse' *casale*, 8, 17-*colonica*, 13; 'small house' *casa*, 8-*domucella*, 25; 'estate' *colonia*, 3, 2-*fundus* and *praedium*, both frequent; 'patrimony' *patrimonium*, 1, 2-*massa*, 1, 13, 2, 17, 10-11; 'vineyard' *vinea*, 20, 10-11-*hortus vineatus*, 17; 'sown fields' *agri arvi*, 10-11-*sationales*, 20), or as they demonstrate a semantic distinction (*casa* 'small house', 8, designation of a *fundus* or *casa*, 8, 17 vs. *domus* 'house', frequent; *caccabellus* and *cucumella*, both 'cook-pots' of different sizes, 8; *ecclesia* 'church', frequent vs. *basilica*, name of a specific church, 8, 17; *dies* 'day', frequent vs. *feria* doubtless 'weekday', less likely as 'holy day', 22). Other items among which grosser distinctions are made in sense are the following: *runcilio* 'pruning hook'-*falx messoria* 'harvest sickle'-*satarium* (?) 'scythe', all in 8; *sagellum* 'travelling coat'—*laena* 'cloak, mantle', both in 8; and *buttis* (for vinegar)-*tina* (closed container for wine)-*cuppus* (probably smaller wine barrel), all in 8. Three gradations in size are doubtless involved in *buttis-buttis minor-butticella*, though it is possible that unlike the other two members the *buttis minor* may not refer to dry measure, see pages 51f.) Finally we note that certain items which we grouped for the purposes of dialectal study actually are not synonymous in our texts, as *campus—terra*, both of which appear in a series in doc. 20, and *desertus*, 3—*incultus*, 10-11, the latter of which refers to the unworked nature of the fields rather than to the fact that they have been abandoned, see pages 62f.

We have touched upon problems involving the sense of *buttis*, etc., above; the most notable observations from the standpoint of the Romance reflexes are that both *buttis* and *butticella* may refer to dry measure, the *tina* is closed, while exact determination of the sense of *cuppus* is not possible, see pages 50, 51, 55. Lastly we note the difficulties associated with the sense of *feria* (see pages 77ff), and also with *sarica*, which in our view has lost its connection with the idea of silk, see page 49. We mention in passing those items whose meaning is corroborated by the evidence of other languages: *mansionarius* (OHG), *statio* (certain Slavic languages), *punga* (Greek or Gothic), and possibly *soca* (doubtless Keltic in origin).

Documents which figure heavily in this discussion are 8 (vessels and containers, field implements, houses), 20 and 10-11 (both involving fields or estates), 17 (houses, churches, and estates), and 1 (new senses which are not continued in the remainder of the collection).

3. *Attestations.* Of all the forms examined, which of course include many CL items, it is remarkable how many items either as forms or examples of change of sense nonetheless are represented in our collection for the first time: (doc. 8, 564) *capsicius, run-*

cilio, punga, soca, sarica and *sareca, caccabellus, butticella;* (25, ca. 600; 21, 625) *horticellus;* (10-11, 489) *notarius* (as 'royal' secretary); (17, beginning of the 7th c.?) *vineatus*. Other items which are possibly antedated by a short period are *bracile* and *cuppus* (both in 8, and both in Isidore), *casalis* (first used as a noun in 8, also in Gregory the Great), while *massa* (1, 445-446; 10-11, 489) is among the first uses of the sense 'patrimony'. Two items which have possibly one earlier occurrence each are *cucumella* and *tina* (both in 8, both before ca. 30 BC). The importance of doc. 8 cannot be too much emphasized: it alone accounts for 75% of these items.

The longevity of our forms is highly variable; we note the following selected examples reflexes of which are extant today in the Romania (including Vegliote): (standard It.) *butticella, feria* (in a compound), *horticellus, mansionarius, massa, notarius* (though not specifically as 'royal' scribe), *potestas, soca, spatharius, testimonium, vineatus;* (It. dialects, widespread) *soca, testimonium,* (N) *notarius* (but not as 'royal' secretary), *butticella, cuppus, casalis* (also southern in different sense), *feria* (in compounds), (N & C) *desertus, incultus,* (N & S) *cucumella, ager,* (S) *caccbellus, cata, punga, terra* (proportionately stronger in the south in comparison with *campus*); (restricted areas of Romania: W. Rheto-Romance) *ager, basilica* (as 'church'), *cuppus, feria, mansionarius, statio,* (Sard.) *bracile* (old Sard.), *cuppus, domus, punga, soca, testimonium,* (Vegliote) *statio,* (Rum.) *basilica* ('church'), *bracile, punga,* (Galicia) *taedium;* (W. Romance:Fr.) *capsicius,* (Port.) *feria,* (Sp.) *spatharius,* (general W. Romance) *cuppus, soca, casalis, testimonium,* (W. Romance and Rum.) *sarica*. Such forms as the following are pan-Romance or at least occur in a very large portion of the Romania: *buttis, tina, campus, casa* (in Fr. in another sense), *ecclesia, dies,* etc. In addition certain items are found largely or wholly in place-names, as: (Italy) *runcilio, cata, domus, massa, casalis,* (elsewhere) *colonia, colonica,* also *casalis*.

In contrast, a number of our items do not survive (except in some cases as place-names just noted) beyond their appearances in earlier stages of Romance, as: *runcilio* (old It.), *armarium* (in the sense "library, archive', N. and C. It.), *necessus* (old Ven., Lomb., Sic.), and elsewhere in Romance, as *sagellum* (old Prov.), *colonica* (old Fr., old Swiss French dialects).

4. *Contributions.* In the course of our previous discussions we have had occasion to indicate discrepancies and matters about which we have disagreed with past scholarship, notable among which are the various treatments of starred forms. Specifically *sarica*, as well as *sareca, bracile*, and *capsicius (-ium?)*, must now be considered as attested on the basis of their appearance in doc. 8. We note of course that the employment of the asterisk has sometimes occurred in works which have been superseded (**bracile* in Puşcariu, **capsiceum* in Gamillscheg, *Etym.*); the one item which has been most consistently thus marked however is *sarica*. We further note that *caccabellus* is attested in works other than our own (as in de Bartholomaeis), while by the precepts of the *FEW*, the form *sagellum* merits a separate entry, rather than being cited with *sagum*, since it is attested as early as the 4th or 5th century. Finally we have pointed out that the two terms *necesse* and *necessus, (-um)* merit separate treatment (unlike *REW* and *DEI*).

With reference to Tjäder's commentary, we point out the following matters which we would amend: *capsicio* is to be associated with Fr. *châssis*, and is treated in *FEW* and Gamillscheg (cf Tjäder, 436, who states that the item is not found in the manuals); *punga* is well attested in Italy (cf Tjäder, 436, who cites the example in doc. 8 as the only one in Italy). Finally we mention his omission of *notarius* which occurs in doc. 22, as well as in the other *loci* noted in Tjäder, 419.

We note in conclusion the following results of our study of correlating the citations in our documents with their subsequent distribution in the Romania. In particular we emphasize the connection with N. Italy as is demonstrated best in the following: *butticella* (also standard It.), *casalis* (also W. Romance), *sationalis* (transmitted mainly by Ravenna texts, survives as adjective only in middle Fr.), *punga* (also elsewhere in It., in the case of Bova most likely an instance of a form which is really Greek), as well as these forms which are attested for the first or almost the first time in the north and which are also widespread in W. Romance (*cuppus, soca, tina*). The association between the following and N. Italy appears less well defined: *potestas* (whose evolution in sense is noted even in CL, but which nonetheless appears in Romance in the 12th c. in C. and N. Italy), *statio* (which appears in both a Ravenna and a Roman text, after first being attested in a variety of locales; the concentration of medieval Latin citations in N. Italy however are doubtless forerunners of the ultimate preservation of the form in N. It. dialects, Rheto-Romance, and Vegliote), and *testimonium* (attested well before our collection in Spain, and later widespread in Italy, Sardinia and W. Romance). A partial correlation is observable in the following in that subsequent attestations appear in C. and N. Italy: *runcilio* (now only in place-names), *armarium* (sense ultimately lost), and *horticellus* (also ultimately standard It.). Finally we point out the significance of items which appear for the first (or almost first) time in our collection but which are later not generally associated with the north; the fact that they now are found in highly conservative regions of the Romania indicates that they were at one time far more widely distributed: *bracile* (Sard., Rum.), *caccabellus* (S. It., old Fr.), and *cucumella* (S. It., and one example in the Pied.).

The following situations are noted between texts in our collection which either do not originate in or which refer to some other region apart from Ravenna: *vineatus* which occurs for the first time in Roman 17 soon appears to progress northward (and is ultimately perhaps the underlying form of certain old Fr. and old Prov. forms); similarly *mansionarius* (Roman 17) is later preserved dialectally in Italy and Rheto-Romance, as well as in W. Romance, in forms which have closely related senses; *massa* which appears in the sense of 'patrimony' in the early texts 1 (which refers to Sicily) and 10-11 (written in Syracuse) nonetheless is later best attested in place-names, many of which are found in N. Italy; *necessus (-um)* (Roman 17) offers little overt connection with later attestations in N. and S. Italy—however it doubtless illustrates that the form was at one time of greater currency. *Notarius* (in Syracuse 10-11) in the sense of 'royal secretary' does not survive later (except possibly in old Fr.), although of course the meaning is a very special application of the more usual 'notary', common in standard It., the N. dialects, and W. Romance, and which likely originated in N. Italy.

Items which appear in our Ravenna texts but which apparently have more affinity with other regions of the Romania are: *sagellum* (old Prov.), and *taedium* (Galician). Similarly *sarica* has descendants in C. and S. Italy, Rum., and Iberia—however not in N. Italy. *Spatharius* occurs only in standard It. and Sp. while *feria* appears most notably in the sense of 'weekday' in Port. and in compounds in standard It. and N. dialects. *Capsicius* survives only in France.

Finally we note in passing that certain CL forms survive very sporadically in the Romania: *ager* (Rheto-Romance, Iberia, and very infrequently in both N. and S. It.), and *domus* (Sard., and place-names in N. and S. Italy). The Greek loan *cata* is similarly frequent in S. It. compounds and place-names; there is no question of a necessary connection with Ravenna inasmuch as the form was long current in Latin before its appearance in our collection.

It has been observed in passing that doc. 8 plays a role of first importance with regard to the lexicon. In certain respects doc. 8 shares a number of features which are characteristic of our collection as a whole (e. g., a widespread use of formulae, fixed pronominal phrases, Germanic names, etc.). However doc. 8 is unique in other respects, not only with regard to the phonology and morphology, mention of which we forego here, but especially with regard to the vocabulary.

The question is of course posed as to 'Why?' this comparative lexical variety in one document alone. In our previous examinations of our collection it was our general policy to approach the data without recourse to external or non-linguistic factors. Our treatment of *punga* (pages 25f) was of course an exception.

In order to answer the question concerning the lexical variety in parts of our collection (which otherwise are quite conservative, at least with regard to spelling aberrations, etc.), we performed the following comparison of the more pertinent lexical items with the great historical events taking place in the regions and at the times of the composition of our texts. Our basic sources are Previté-Orton and to lesser extent works by Vasiliev and Migliorini. We emphasize (by italicizing) especially those terms which appear formally or semantically for the first (or almost first) time in our collection. (In the interests of completeness we also mention peripherally those items which we had occasion to remark upon in the preceding discussion.) The historical outline is based primarily upon the ruling forces in power in Italy in the course of the time represented by our collection (445-700). The following table is a chronological listing of our individual texts; as for the subject matter of the documents, mixed topics prevail in the 5th and 6th centuries while in the 7th century we find exclusively donations (docs. 16 through 23, including Roman 17 and 18-19), compare our remarks on pages 11f.

THE ROMAN EMPIRE

1. *Division of the E. and W. Roman Empire:* After the division of the Empire into two parts (364), Honorius, alarmed by German incursions in the north, transfers the imperial court to Ravenna (404).

Doc. 1 (445-446): *massa 'patrimony'*, taedium 'illness', testimonium 'witness'.

Doc. 4-5: 4th W (before 474): potestas 'praetorian prefect'.

THE GERMANS

2. *Fall of the W. Roman Empire:* With the deposal of Romulus Augustulus, Odoacer, the head of German mercenaries, names himself ruler of Italy (including Sicily which is ceded to him) (476); however he makes no claim to the title of emperor of the west.

Doc. 4-5: 3rd W (480).

Doc. 10-11 (Syracuse, 489): massa, *notarius 'royal scribe'*, (ager arvus, incultus, necesse, vinea).

3. *The Ostrogoths:* Ravenna which falls (493) to Theodoric becomes the seat of the Ostrogothic domain until 526.

Doc. 4-5: 5th W (520-521).

THE BYZANTINES

4. *Attempts on the part of the E. Empire at reunification of the Empire:* Belisarius, a general of Justinian the eastern emperor, defeats the Vandals in N. Africa (533), invades Sicily in 535 (which is however ultimately subdued only by Narses who defeats Totila, the Ostrogothic general, in 550), takes Naples and Rome (536), and in 540 captures Ravenna, which becomes the seat of Byzantine power in Italy (see also page 25).

Doc. 4-5: 6th W (552).

Doc. 4-5: Concl. portion (552): notarius 'church scribe', potestas 'praetorian prefect'.

Doc. 13 (553): (colonica 'farmhouse', potestas 'power').

Doc. 3 (mid-6th c. ?): (colonia 'farm', desertus 'abandoned').

Doc. 7 (Rieti, 557).

Doc. 8 (564): *bracile, butticella, caccabellus,* casa, *casalis* (as noun), *capsicius, cucumella, cup(p)us, punga, runcilio, sagellum, sarica* and *sareca, soca, tina* (and buttis, basilica, domus, fundus, praedium).

Doc. 2 (565-570): potestas 'praetorian prefect'.

Doc. 14-15 (572).

Doc. 6 (575): cata, statio; (deposition in Greek characters).

5. *The Exarchate of Ravenna:* The Exarchate is mentioned for the first time (584); it is an administrative province of the Byzantine domain in Italy and until the middle of the 7th century it is comprised of Istria, Venetia, Emilia with Ravenna, the Pentapolis consisting of five cities on the east coast, from Ravenna to south of Ancona, Calabria (then the "heel" of Italy), Bruttium (the "toe"), Naples and S. Campania, Rome and N. Campania, S. Tuscany, Perugia, and Liguria.

Doc. 20 (590-602?): (campus, potestas 'power', sationales, terra, vinea); (also a deposition in Greek characters).

Doc. 16 (ca. 600?): potestas 'office of the praetorian prefect', spatharius (in the signature of witnesses); (deposition in Greek characters).

Doc. 17 (Rome, beginning of the 7th c. ?): mansionarius, necessus (-um), *vineatus* (also basilica, casa, casalis).

Doc. 18-19 (Rome, beginning of the 7th c. ?): statio; (deposition in Greek characters).

Doc. 25 (ca. 600): domucella, *horticellus*.

Doc. 28 (613-641).

Doc. 21 (625): *horticellus*, notarius 'church scribe'.

Doc. 22 (639): armarium, feria, notarius 'church scribe'.

Doc. 24 (mid-7th c. ?): (Deposition in Greek characters).

Doc. 23 (ca. 700).

6. *The loss of Byzantine Ravenna:* Ravenna is lost (751) to the Lombards, who in turn give way to the Franks under Pippin who donates the Exarchate to Pope Stephen II (756).

Two facts are immediately apparent from the foregoing: 1) doc. 8 which contains nearly all of the neologisms occurs very shortly after the Byzantine conquest of Ravenna, while 2) the great bulk of the later documents (from both Ravenna and Rome) are apparently written well after the establishment of Byzantine political and cultural influence. We have noted above the various texts which contain one deposition each written by a witness who while writing Latin expressed himself by means of Greek characters. We further point out such names and terms of Greek origin as appear in 18-19 (written in Rome, which was at that time in the sphere of Byzantine influence) and 20 (respectively *Chrisogonus* and *hypodecta*). This tendency on the part of a small but significant number of witnesses who in many cases were not well educated bespeaks a certain cultural awareness (though in at least one instance the witness is a Syrian who doubtless had no other choice, in doc. 20).

While the papacy especially as represented by Gregory the Great (590-603) was pre-eminent in Rome and its environs, even to the point where officials appointed by the Exarch for the duchy of Rome were subservient (cf Previté-Orton, 223f), it is apparent from our Roman documents that Rome as well as Ravenna was very much under the influence of the cultural force of Byzantium. For example, we note in the case of doc. 18-19 that the donor (Stephanus) is himself a Greek (from Naples) who is making his gift to the *Ravenna* church. Furthermore, while doc. 18-19 accounts for certain phonological changes, which we shall not go into here, and displays a certain distinctiveness, it is apparent that the text, along with doc. 17, also from Rome, is totally typical in its make-up to the whole class of documents which comprise the donations.

We refer to the table in Tjäder, 257, in which the very complete attestation in both documents of the various formularistic patterns which characterize all of the donations is graphically depicted. Thus the two documents (and especially 18-19 with its pro-Ravenna orientation) are part and parcel of the whole scribal tradition which we associate with Ravenna, cf Tjäder, 146f.

Other evidences of the cultural activity manifested by the Byzantines are only too well known: the 6th c. mosaics, as well as the church building activity (especially under Justinian who in several cases continued works begun by the Ostrogoths), cf Vasiliev, 190f, and also 128. While we shall not pursue in detail the matter of varying quality of the documents (some of which differences may be attributed to ignorance on the part of the witnesses), we refer merely to Tjäder's remarks which precede each text. We note by way of example that doc. 16 (which appears above among the donations, in our last time group) is classed as perhaps one of the most beautiful examples of the Latin papyri in Italy, cf E. Monaci, in *Archivio paleografico italiano*, vol. I, Rome, 1882-1897.

Precisely because of the strong cultural influence of Byzantium a case can be made for the preservation for the most part of a CL tradition. It is seemingly paradoxical, but the situation is quite comparable to the case of the foreigner who has mastered a second language to the point that he is doubtless superior, from a puristic standpoint, in his ability to that of the native speaker.

This linguistic conservatism is further enhanced by the widespread use of fixed phrases, clichés, formulae. By way of example, we cite almost at random these versions of a *dolus malus* clause: *huic tam legaliter pefecte donationi dolum malum abesse afuturumque esse promittimus* (doc. 13), *absque ullo dolo malo, vim, metu et circumscribtione cassante* (16), *quam donationis meae paginam omni vi, dolo, metu et circumscriptione cessante* (20), and *cui rei dolum malum abesse afuturumque esse promitto* (NR-18-19). Indeed it is virtually impossible to examine our documents without being struck by the profusion of formularistic expressions. However, rarely are the expressions mere repetitions of each other (as may in fact occur in the case of witnesses all giving the same deposition); we see rather series of reworkings and variations performed about a central notion and usually within the limitations of a fairly fixed total number of lexical items at the disposal of the scribe. In short, our scribes are familiar with models whose essence they adhere to, all the while adding some small personal feature. Knowledge of these key notions was possibly transmitted orally, although we cannot discount a written tradition, given the obvious cultural disposition of the Byzantine scribes. We might compare such use of the partially fixed expresion with the well known examples of variations on formulae types of the old French epics, as described for example in Rychner, 141ff. Nonetheless a difference remains: while the tradition of the narrators of the epics was an oral one, and one which depended upon getting over to the listener a relatively detailed story by means of subtle and repeated re-workings of the essential features, that of our scribes is 1) bound up with a legalistic tradition, and 2) allows of variation only in the very circumscribed limitations of the legal point being made.

This same conservatism of expression is further apparent in the vocabulary of the last group of texts examined above, for as we have indicated very few neologisms appear *(horticellus, vineatus)*. Doc. 8 which appears chronologically somewhat earlier must therefore simply be considered as one highly individualistic, atypical text which represents a cultural break-through far in advance of its time but which is nonetheless confirmed by successive developments in Romance. Thus, while doc. 8 is also well represented in formulae, like the rest of our collection, it must be realized that this is true only in the first portion of the text (we ignore of course the signatures at the end). It is precisely in the second paragraph which consists of listings of individual items, as in an inventory, that our neologisms are found. Thus the scribe, who now has no recourse either to a formularized model, or for that matter to a classical lexicon, is free to employ those terms which doubtless more accurately reflect the actual word stock then prevalent in the speech of Ravenna. While most of the neologisms are based on CL, *punga* and *soca,* both of which are certainly from foreign or substratum sources, may also indicate the presence of other non-Latin speech elements. It is in this sense that the second paragraph of doc. 8, once freed from any dependence upon a formularistic model (which necessarily cannot exist in the case of listings), is the best representation in our collection of "popular" speech.

As for certain of the other texts which vary considerably as to overall subject matter, doc. 1 which is by far our earliest text seems to participate in the case of *testimonium* in what must have been a widespread use of the term as 'witness' (compare the *Peregrinatio* which considerably antedates our text). Docs. 17 and 10-11 (both of which are non-Ravenna) appear prominently in our study of the lexicon, however chiefly with reference to the geographical distribution of terms for 'fields', 'estates', etc. Interestingly, doc. 7 (also non-Ravenna) does not figure in our study of the lexicon at all.

One further distinction may be made with regard to the overall make-up of our collection: whereas the signatures of witnesses account inordinately for spelling aberrations (for details of which cf Tjäder, 148ff), they are represented almost not at all in the neologisms (the one exception is *spatharius,* doc. 16).

It remains for doc. 8, despite the fact that it is not chronologically the latest text in our collection, to give a preview of some highly interesting lexical items which as early as 564 point the way to subsequent developments in Romance.

BIBLIOGRAPHY

Certain of our sources are identified in our text by the following designations (we omit here the more obvious ones). Furthermore, in our text, references are always to pages, not paragraphs, with the one exception being REW where the numbers refer to items. "P." under the AIS entries refers to points on maps.

AGI — *Archivio glottologico italiano.*
AIS — Jaberg and Jud, *Sprach- und Sachatlas Italiens und der Südschweiz.*
ASI — *Archivio storico italiano.*
CGL — *Corpus glossariorum Latinorum.*
CIL — *Corpus inscriptionum Latinarum.*
Corom. — Corominas, *Diccionario crítico etimológico.*
DEI — Battisti and Alessio, *Dizionario etimologico italiano.*
DES — Wagner, *Dizionario etimologico sardo.*
DRG — *Dicziunari rumantsch-grischun.*
Du Cange—see *Glossarium... latinitatis... Carolo du Fresne domino du Cange....*
FEW — von Wartburg, *Französisches etymologisches Wörterbuch.*
GGA — *Göttingsche Gelehrte Anzeigen.*
GLE — Sella, *Glossario latino emiliano.*
GLI — Sella, *Glossario latino italiano.*
RE — see *Paulys Real-Encyclopädie...*
REW — Meyer-Lübke, *Romanisches etymologisches Wörterbuch.*
ThesLL — *Thesaurus linguae latinae.*

* * *

ALCOVER SUREDA, A. M., ed. *Diccionari Català-Valencià-Balear...*, continued by Francesc de B. Moll, Palma de Mallorca, 1930- .
Archiv für lateinische Lexicographie und Grammatik, Leipzig, 1884- .
Archivio glottologico italiano, Turin-Rome, 1873- .
Archivio storico italiano, Florence, 1842- .
Archivum Romanicum, Geneva-Florence, 1917-1941.
ARNALDI, F., *Latinitatis italicae medii aevi inde a. CDLXXLI usque ad a. MXXII lexicon imperfectum*, in *Archivum Latinitatis medii Aevi*, vols. 10 (1936), 12 (1938), 20 (1950), 21 (1951), 23 (1953), 27 (1957), 28 (1958), 29 (1959), 32 (1962), Brussels.
BARCIANU, S. P., *Vocabulariu romanu-nemtiescu*, Sibiiu, 1868.

BATTISTI, C., and ALESSIO, G., *Dizionario etimologico italiano*, 5 vols., Florence, 1950-1957.
BAXTER, J. H., and JOHNSON, C., *Medieval Latin Word-List*, London, 1950.
BERTONI, G., *Italia dialettale*, Milano, 1916.
BLAISE, A., *Dictionnaire latin-français des auteurs chrétiens*, Strasbourg, 1954.
BLATT, FR., *Novum Glossarium mediae Latinitatis ab anno DCCC usque ad annum MCC*, Copenhagen, 1957-
BONNET, M., *Le latin de Grégoire de Tours*, Paris, 1890.
BOSSHARD, H., *Saggio di un glossario dell'antico lombardo, compilato su statuti e altre carte medievali della Lombardia e della Svizzera italiana*, Florence, 1938, in *Biblioteca dell 'Archivum Romanicum'*, ser. 2, vol. 23.
BOURCIEZ, Ed., *Eléments de linguistique romane*, 4th ed., Paris, 1946.
BRUPPACHER, H. P., *Die Namen der Wochentage im Italienischen und Rätoromanischen*, Bern, 1948, in *Romanica Helvetica*, vol. 28.
CABROL, F., *Dictionnaire d'archéologie chrétienne et de liturgie*, Paris, 1907-.
CASTRO, A., *Glosarios latino-españoles de la edad media*, Madrid, 1936.
CIONARESCU, A., *Diccionario etimológico rumano*, La Laguna, 1958-
COOPER, F. T., *Word Formation in the 'Roman Sermo Plebeius'*, New York, 1895.
COROMINAS, J., *Diccionario crítico etimológico de la lengua castellana*, 4 vols., Bern, 1954.
Corpus glossariorum Latinorum, ed. G. Loewe, G. Goetz, vols. 1-7, Leipzig-Berlin, 1888-1923.
Corpus inscriptionum Latinarum, Berlin, 1863.
DE CIHAC, A., *Dictionnaire d'étymologie daco-romane*, Frankfurt, 1879.
Dicziunari rumantsch-grischun, Cuoria, 1939-
DIEHL, E., *Inscriptiones Latinae Christianae Veteres*, vols. 1-3, Berlin, 1925, 1927, 1931.
DIEZ, FR., *Etymologisches Wörterbuch der romanischen Sprachen*, 4th ed., Bonn, 1878.
DIEFENBACH, L., *Vergleichendes Wörterbuch der gotischen Sprache*, 2 vols., Frankfurt, 1851.
Dizionario enciclopedico italiano, Rome, 1955-
ECKHARDT, K. A., *Lex Salica, 100 Titel-Text*, Weimar, 1953.
Enciclopedia cattolica. Città del Vaticano, 1949-1954.
Enciclopedia italiana di scienze, lettere ed arti..., 36 vols., Rome, 1929-1939.
ERNOUT, A., *Aspects du vocabulaire latin*, Paris, 1954.
ERNOUT, A., and MEILLET, A., *Dictionnaire étymologique de la langue latine*, 2 vols., 4th ed., Paris, 1960.
ESTIENNE, H., *Thesaurus Graecae Linguae*, Paris, 1831-65.
FACCIOLATI, J., and FORCELLINI, E., *Lexicon totius latinitatis*, Padua, 1864.
———, *Onomasticon*, Padua, 1864.
FEIST, S., *Etymologisches Wörterbuch der gotischen Sprache*, Halle, 1909.
———, *Vergleichendes Wörterbuch der gotischen Sprache*, 3rd ed., Leyden, 1939.
FORCELLINI, E., *Totius latinitatis lexicon*, 6 vols., Prati, 1858-1875.
FREUND, W., *Grand dictionnaire de la langue latine*, Paris, 1883.
GAMILLSCHEG, E., *Etymologisches Wörterbuch der französischen Sprache*, Heidelberg, 1928.
———, *Romania Germanica*, Berlin-Leipzig, 1935, in *Grundriss der Germanischen Philologie*, vol. 11, part 2.

GARCÍA DE DIEGO, V., *Diccionario etimológico español e hispánico*, Madrid, 1954.
GIRY, A., *Manuel de diplomatique*, Paris, 1894.
Glossaire des patois de la Suisse romande, founded by L. Gauchat, J. Jeanjaquet and E. Tappolet, Neuchâtel-Paris, 1924- .
Glossarium mediae et infimae latinitatis conditum a Carolo du Fresne domino du Cange... digessit G. A. L. Henschel, vols. 1-10, Paris, 1937.
Glotta, Zeitschrift für griechische und lateinische Sprache, Göttingen, 1909-.
GODEFROY, F. E., *Dictionnaire de l'ancienne langue française*, 10 vols., Paris, 1880-1902.
Göttingsche Gelehrte Anzeigen, Göttingen, 1739-.
GRANDGENT, C. H., *An Introduction to Vulgar Latin*, Boston, 1907.
————, *From Latin to Italian*, Cambridge, 1940.
GROSSI-GONDI, F., *Trattato di epigrafia cristiana latina e greca*, Rome, 1920.
HABEL, E., and GRÖBEL, F., *Mittellateinisches Glossar*, 2nd ed., Paderborn, 1959.
HAKAMIES, R., *Glossarium Latinitatis Medii Aevi Finlandicae*, Helsinki, 1958.
HASSELROT, B., *Etudes sur la formation diminutive dans les langues romanes*, in *Uppsala Universitets Arsskrift*, vol. 11, 1957.
HAUST, J., *Etymologies wallonnes et françaises*, Liège, 1923.
HEUMANN, J., *Handlexicon zu den Quellen des römischen Rechts*, revised by E. Seckel, 9th ed., Jena, 1926.
HILL, J. M., *"Universal vocabulario" de Alfonso de Palencia*, Madrid, 1957.
L'Italia dialettale. Rivista di dialettologia italiana diretta da Clemente Merlo... Pisa, 1925- .
JABERG, K., and JUD, J., *Index zum Sprach- und Sachatlas Italiens und der Südschweiz...*, Bern, 1960.
————, *Sprach- und Sachatlas Italiens und der Südschweiz*, Zofingen, 1928-1940.
Jagić-Festschrift, Zbornik u slavu V. Jagiča, Berlin, 1908
JOSEPHSON, Å., *Casae litterarum*, Uppsala, 1950.
JUD, J., *Zur Geschichte der bündner-romanischen Kirchensprache*, Chur, 1919.
KLUGE, F., *Etymologisches Wörterbuch der deutschen Sprache*, 17th ed., Berlin, 1957.
KÖRTING, G., *Etymologisches Wörterbuch der französischen Sprache*, Paderborn, 1908.
————, *Lateinisch-romanisches Wörterbuch*, 3rd ed., Paderborn, 1907.
Lesicon Románescu-Látinescu-Ungurescu-Nemțescu... seu Lexicon Valachico-Latino-Hungarico-Germanicum..., Buda, 1825.
LEVY, EM., *Provenzalisches Supplement Wörterbuch*, 8 vols., Leipzig, 1894-1924.
LEVY, E., *West Roman Vulgar Law. The Law of Property*, Philadelphia, 1951, in *Memoirs of the American Philosophical Society*, vol. 29.
LEWIS, C. T., and SHORT, CH., *A Latin Dictionary*, Oxford, 1879.
LEWY, H. and J., *The Week and the oldest west Asiatic Calendar*, Cincinnati, 1943, in *Hebrew Union College Annual*, vol. 17.
LIDDELL-SCOTT, *Greek-English Lexicon*, rev. by H. S. Jones, Oxford, 1925.
LÖFSTEDT, B., *Studien über die Sprache der langobardischen Gesetze*, Uppsala, 1961, in *Acta Universitatis Upsaliensis, Studia Latina Upsaliensia*, vol. 1.
Löfstedt, Ei., *Late Latin*, Oslo 1959.
————, *Philologischer Kommentar zur Peregrinatio Aetheriae*, Uppsala, 1911.

LÖFSTEDT, EI., *Syntactica. Studien und Beiträge zur historischen Syntax des Lateins*, Lund, 2nd ed., 1956, in *Skrifter utgivna av Kungl. Humanistiska Vetenskapssamfundet i Lund*, vols. 10: 1, 10: 2.

──────, *Vermischte Studien zur lateinischen Sprachkunde und Syntax*, Lund, 1936, in *Skrifter utgivna av Kungl. Humanistiska Vetenskapssamfundet i Lund*, vol. 23.

LORCK, J. E., *Altbergamaskische Sprachdenkmäler*, Halle, 1893.

MAIGNE D'ARNIS, W. H., *Lexicon manuale ad scriptores mediae et infimae latinitatis*, Paris, 1890.

MENÉNDEZ-PIDAL, R., *Manual de gramática histórica española*, Madrid, 1941.

MEYER, G., *Neugriechischen Studien*, Vienna, 1895.

MEYER-LÜBKE, W., *Grammaire des langues romanes*, 4 vols., Paris, 1890-1906.

──────, *Romanisches etymologisches Wörterbuch*, 3rd ed., Heidelberg, 1935.

MIGLIORINI, B., *Storia della lingua italiana*, Florence, 1960.

MISTRAL, F., *Lou tresor dóu Felibrige, ou dictionnaire provençal-français*, 2 vols., Aix-en-Provence, 1878-1887.

Mittellateinisches Wörterbuch bis zum ausgehenden 13. Jahrhundert..., Munich, 1959-

MOHRMANN, CHR., "*Statio*", Amsterdam, 1953, in *Vigiliae Christianae. A Review of Early Christian Life and Language*, vol. 7.

MONACI, E., *Crestomazia italiana dei primi secoli...*, revised ed., Rome, 1955.

MONLAU Y ROCA, P. F., *Diccionario etimológico de la lengua castellana*, 2nd ed., Buenos Aires, 1944.

DE MORAIS E SILVA, A., *Grande dicionário da língua portuguesa*, 12 vols. 10th ed., Lisbon, 1949.

MULLER, Fr., *Altitalisches Wörterbuch*, Göttingen, 1926.

NETTLESHIP, H., *Contributions to Latin Lexicography*, Oxford, 1889.

NIERMEYER, J. F., *Mediae Latinitatis Lexicon minus*, Leyden, 1954-

OLIVIERI, D., *Dizionario etimologico italiano*, Milan, 1953.

PACE, B., *Arte e civiltà della Sicilia antica*, vol. 4, Rome-Naples-Città di Castello, 1949.

PAIVA BOLÉO, M. DE, *Os nomes dos dias da semana em português*, Coimbra, 1941.

Paulys Real-Encyclopädie der classischen Altertumswissenschaft, Stuttgart, 1894-

PEI, M., *The Language of the Eighth-Century Texts in Northern France*, New York, 1932.

POLITZER, R. L., *A Study of the Language of Eighth Century Lombardic Documents*, New York, 1949.

POLITZER, R. L., and POLITZER, F. N., *Romance Trends in 7th and 8th Century Latin Documents*, Chapel Hill, 1953, in *University of North Carolina Studies in the Romance Languages and Literatures*, vol. 21.

PRATI, A., *Vocabolario etimologico italiano*, Milan, 1951.

PREVITÉ-ORTON, C. W., *The Shorter Cambridge Medieval History*, vol. 1, Cambridge, 1960.

PUŞCARIU, S., *Etymologisches Wörterbuch der rumänischen Sprache*, vol. 1, Heidelberg, 1905.

RAČKI, FR., *Documenta historiae Chroaticae periodum antiquam illustrantia...*, Zagreb, 1877, in *Monumenta spectantia historiam Slavorum Meridionalium...*, vol. 7.

RAYNOUARD, FR. J. M., *Lexique roman ou dictionnaire de la langue des troubadours*, 6 vols., Paris, 1838-1844.

ROHLFS, G., *Ager, area, atrium*, Borna-Leipzig, 1920.
———, "*Baskische Kultur im Spiegel des lateinischen Lehnwortes*", in *Philologische Studien aus dem romanisch-germanischen Kulturkreise. Karl Voretzsch zum 60. Geburtstag...*, Halle, 1927.
———, "*Die Lexikalische Differenzierung der romanischen Sprachen*", in *Sitzungsberichte der Bayerischen Akademie der Wissenschaften. Philosophisch-historische Klasse*, vol. 4, Munich, 1954.
———, *Dizionario dialettale delle tre Calabrie*, 3 vols., Halle-Milan, 1932, 1934, 1939.
———, "*Germanisches Spracherbe in der Romania*", in *Sitzungsberichte der Bayerischen Akademie der Wissenschaften*, Munich, 1944-1946, vol. 8.
———, *Historische Grammatik der italienischen Sprache und ihrer Mundarten*, 3 vols., Bern, 1949-1953.
Romania, Paris, 1872- .
RYCHNER, J., *La Chanson de geste*, Geneva-Lille, 1955.
SCHADE, O., *Altdeutsches Wörterbuch*, 2 vols., Halle, 1872-1882.
SCHEUERMEIER, P., *Bauernwerk in Italien...*, vol. 1, Erlenbach-Zürich, 1943.
SCHMID, J., *Handwörterbuch des Kirchenlateins*, Limburg/Lahn, 1934.
SCHULZE, E., *Gothisches Wörterbuch*, Züllichau, 1867.
SELLA, P., *Glossario latino emiliano*, Città di Vaticano, 1937, in *Biblioteca Vaticana, Studi e testi*, n.º 74.
———, *Glossario latino italiano*, Città del Vaticano, 1944, in *Biblioteca Vaticana, Studi e testi*, n.º 109.
SERRA, G., *La tradizione latina e greco-latina nell'onomastica medioevale italiana*, Gothenburg, 1949, in *Göteborgs Högskolas Årsskrift*, vol. 55, part 2.
SKEAT, W. W., *An Etymological Dictionary of the English Language*, Oxford, 1882.
SLEUMER, A., *Kirchenlateinisches Wörterbuch*, Limburg/Lahn, 1926.
Słownik łaciny średniowiecznej w Polsce. Lexicon mediae et infimae latinitatis Polonorum, Polska Akademia Nauk, Warsaw, 1953- .
SOPHOCLES, E. A., *Greek Lexicon of the Roman and Byzantine Periods from BC 146 to AD 1100*, 2 vols., reprinted, New York, 1957.
SOUTER, A., *A Glossary of later Latin to 600 A. D.*, Oxford, 1949.
STOLZ-SCHMALZ, *Lateinische Grammatik. Laut- und Formenlehre. Syntax und Stilistik*, 5th ed., revised by M. Leumann and J. B. Hofmann, Munich, 1926.
STRECKER, K., *Introduction to Medieval Latin*, revised and translated by R. B. Palmer, Berlin, 1957.
SVENNUNG, J., *Wortstudien zu den spätlateinischen Oribasiusrezensionen*, Uppsala, 1933, in *Uppsala Universitets Årsskrift*, vol. 33, part 3.
Thesaurus linguae latinae..., Leipzig, 1900- .
THURNEYSEN, R., *Keltoromanisches*, Halle, 1884.
TOBLER, A., and LOMMATZSCH, E., *Altfranzösisches Wörterbuch*, Berlin, 1925.
TRAINA, A., *Nuovo vocabolario siciliano-italiano*, Palermo, 1868.
VASILIEV, A. A., *History of the Byzantine Empire, 324-1453*, Madison, 1952.
VINCENT, A., *Toponymie de la France*, Brussels, 1937.
WAGNER, M. L., *Dizionario etimologico sardo*, Heidelberg, 1957- .
WALDE, A., *Lateinisches etymologisches Wörterbuch*, 3rd ed., revised by J. B. Hofmann, Heidelberg, 1938.
WARTBURG, W. VON, *Französisches etymologisches Wörterbuch*, Bonn, 1922-.

WARTBURG, W. VON, *"Los nombres de los días de la semana"*, Revista de filología española, vol. 33, 1949, Madrid.

WENGER, L., *Die Quellen des römischen Rechts*, Vienna, 1953, in Österreichische Akademie der Wissenschaften, Denkschriften der Gesamtakademie, vol. 2.

Zeitschrift für deutsche Wortforschung, Strasbourg, 1900- .

Zeitschrift für französische Sprache und Litteratur, Jena-Leipzig, 1879- .

Zeitschrift für romanische Philologie, Halle-Tübingen, 1877- .

The Department of Romance Studies Digital Arts and Collaboration Lab at the University of North Carolina at Chapel Hill is proud to support the digitization of the North Carolina Studies in the Romance Languages and Literatures series.

www.ingramcontent.com/pod-product-compliance
Lightning Source LLC
Chambersburg PA
CBHW020421230426
43663CB00007BA/1264